# My Story

# My Story

A Personal Journey

∞

Bonnie Colleen Leininger

Copyright © 2011 by Bonnie Colleen Leininger.

| Library of Congress Control Number: | | 2011915470 |
|---|---|---|
| ISBN: | Hardcover | 978-1-4653-5724-3 |
| | Softcover | 978-1-4653-5723-6 |
| | Ebook | 978-1-4653-5725-0 |

All rights reserved. No part of this book may be reproduced or transmitted in any form or by any means, electronic or mechanical, including photocopying, recording, or by any information storage and retrieval system, without permission in writing from the copyright owner.

This book was printed in the United States of America.

**To order additional copies of this book, contact:**
Xlibris Corporation
1-888-795-4274
www.Xlibris.com
Orders@Xlibris.com

# ACKNOWLEDGMENTS

First AND FOREMOST, I want to thank my devoted husband, Don. I am so grateful for his unselfish commitment. He shared this journey with me and kept me balanced in my darkest times. As I wrote about my life battling with multiple sclerosis (MS), he listened, read, and reread my notes and pages as I put all of my thoughts on paper.

There were numerous nights when he would awaken to find me missing from our bedroom. He would search the recesses of the house and find me wrapped to my neck in an afghan with my laptop propped on my knees and our pup, Finnegan, curled up beside me.

When my memory failed me and dates were muddled, he would remind me of an episode I may have forgotten. If it wasn't for Don's recall, I wouldn't have remembered those small, less-than-significant events that filled the gaps in our lives as we raised our children and kept our houses in working order.

My sons played an important role in editing my thoughts for this book as well. They remembered the funny periods, proven to be the foundation that held our family together, when my outlook was bleak and I needed to laugh.

My oldest son, Don Jr. (DJ), whom I have referenced many times in this book, has created a foundation to honor the twenty-fourth anniversary of my MS diagnosis.

The Team 24/Seven Foundation was created not only to honor me but also to reflect on MS. As my son explains, multiple sclerosis is a 24/7 disease. Those who are affected by MS live with it every hour of every day of their lives. There are very promising new drugs being developed to combat the devastating effects of multiple sclerosis, but as yet, there is still no cure.

Each year, the foundation will sponsor an event that will offer help to a family who has shown the same determination and grit that DJ witnessed in his own family. He knows from experience that multiple sclerosis affects not just the individual but the family unit as well. To beat the disease, it takes a team effort.

The foundation's first fund-raising event took place on Labor Day weekend, 2011. DJ left his home in Harrisburg, Pennsylvania, on September 2 and walked to our home in Reading in twenty-four hours. This was a daunting seventy-mile trek. He had been training for this event for well over a year.

My book is dedicated in part to the unending time and effort that my son is taking to support and aid those families who are struggling with the daily demands of life with multiple sclerosis.

Thank you, DJ, from the bottom of my heart. You grew up to be a wonderful, loving, intelligent young man. I hope that your inspiration for the foundation came not only from me but also from your father's diligence and determination as he held our family together in the face of this catastrophic and crippling disease.

# *AUTHOR'S NOTE*

EXCEPT FOR MY family, I chose not to use the actual names of any of the physicians or others whom I have referenced in my story. I felt it was not my right to authenticate their personalities. Each of them helped in their own way, taking me to the next level in my battle with MS. I appreciate all the hands-on help, encouragement, and support from my friends and caregivers. I will always be grateful because without their assistance, my family would surely have struggled to keep pace with all the changes that took place in our lives.

I never envisioned this narrative to actually be bound and shelved in a bookstore. The original intent was to compile all the fragmented stories surrounding my years of dealing with multiple sclerosis. As the story developed, I realized that my words may lend support to others who are newly diagnosed with MS. Whether because they themselves are afflicted or someone close to them has the disease, I know firsthand the trepidation that they are dealing with and the many unanswered questions that they ask.

Although there are multitudes of books on the market that state the obvious effects, causes, and conditions surrounding MS,

I think that it is important to also share the human aspect, to tell the day-to-day disillusionments and triumphant times as well. My mission in writing **My** *Story: A Personal Journey* is to ease the mind of that person who struggles with the mental anguish of having multiple sclerosis. If I can help just one person, then I will feel my own fight took on greater meaning.

I realize that there is a very real need to share my journey with others. I felt the same insecurities as many of these men and women. I asked the same questions and was as frightened of the long-term effects. I know that some feel they have nowhere to turn for answers.

It took me almost fifteen years to muster the courage to join a support group. I was so fearful of what I would encounter there. I did not want to see the inevitability of the disease. These meetings would have allayed many of my fears, but I had no one to help me see the benefits of belonging to such a group. I want others to feel comfortable sharing their personal experiences and learn from those who have the same difficulties.

The frustration that I felt with multiple sclerosis was reduced considerably when I accepted the challenges of the disease and shared my story with others. The last twenty-four years has been a whirlwind of highs and lows for me. Hopefully, by speaking out, I can reduce the time that others will expend coming to grips with MS.

My contact information is available on my website, www.MSCares.net.

I encourage anyone who has doubts or anxious moments to please contact me directly through my site.

# PROLOGUE

*January 2011*

"... AND THAT, MY friends, is the mind-set one must have in order to beat this disease."

It is mid-January, and I have been traveling throughout the country giving my motivational speech to those with multiple sclerosis and to their caring family and friends who join them.

Tonight, as in the past, the auditorium rose to its feet in applause at the end of my presentation. It warms me to know that I have hopefully helped ease someone's uncertainty about this disease. At one time, I was in the same situation as many in this audience. I was newly diagnosed with a dreadful illness and didn't know where to turn for information or guidance.

I studied the faces of my listeners throughout my presentation. I saw optimism in those who now discover a new dynamic for dealing with MS. They learned that their perception of the disease is the difference between acceptance and despair. I hope that I have given them the tools that they will need to move forward in their lives. I am gratified to know that I broke through and, maybe in a small way, saved a family from self-destruction.

The other part of my audience, however, still exhibits fear and foreboding. They know their lives have been irrevocably altered, and it terrifies them. The discovery of MS stopped their world, and they fear that their way of life will never be the same. I invite them to ask me questions, to tell me why MS is causing such anxiety for them; what is it that they fear most?

The purpose of my program is to open the minds of these individuals. I want them to realize that life can be just as fulfilling for them as before their diagnosis; to rid them of the fear of not knowing what will happen next. Some of whom I've spoken to are hoping for an intervention. They wish to find the missing piece that they believe will fit and help to make them complete again.

George Bernard Shaw, one of the greatest playwrights of our time, once said, "People are always blaming their circumstances for what they are. I don't believe in circumstances. The people who get on in this world are the people who get up and look for the circumstances they want and if they can't find them, make them."

The point that I make to my audience is to keep fighting. Don't let their current situation defeat them. Never accept circumstances that drag them backward. This begins with a strong mental attitude. Like any disease, a person with MS has to fight back every day.

There may come a time when their stamina slides and they don't feel that they have the mental fortitude to fight anymore. This is the day that they have to reach deep inside themselves and believe that they are not going to let multiple sclerosis beat them. Each time that they pull themselves back up to battle another day, they will know that they are stronger than their illness.

# MY STORY

I tell my audiences that a person is multifaceted, and what they are dealing with is only a small part of who they are. Unfortunately, the negative connotation of MS still prevails. Their doctors, albeit unintentionally, have explained the diagnosis and prognosis in such defeating terms that all they can foresee is a catastrophic life sentence with no hope of parole from a wheelchair.

I speak from experience. Twenty-four years ago, a doctor told me that I had multiple sclerosis. He suggested that I build a one-story house and have the doorways widened to fit my eventual wheelchair. I didn't listen.

Blessed with determination and the love and great support of my family and friends, I overcame the worse of this disease. This is my story.

# CHAPTER ONE

*September 1974*

THE WEATHER WAS unusually crisp for late September. Don and I had just moved into a new apartment complex in a suburb of Pittsburgh. We wanted to settle in before the trees would shed their leaves and be replaced with the icy coating of winter. Our furnishings were meager: several mismatched pieces in the bedroom, a sofa, and two bookcases filled with college texts. In the corner sat a leaf-starved rubber tree plant. Life was good, and our plans together were illimitable.

Our first big purchase as newlyweds was a 1964 MG Midget. "Zelda" was a temperamental gal. Too warm and she would overheat; too wet and she would short out; too cold in the mornings and Zelda sat in our apartment's lot waiting for the sun's rays to warm her engine.

Coming home from work one evening, the MG's engine decided to freeze in the middle of a busy road. Struggling to climb the hill, she stubbornly chugged to a stop. I was nowhere near home. I walked over half a mile before I found a phone to call for a tow truck. Unfortunately, cell phones were not an option in those days!

That evening, I noticed a strange sensation in the soles of my feet. Although they felt a normal temperature to the touch, internally, they were on fire! By the middle of the night, I could only find relief by standing on the cold tile floor in our bathroom.

What did I expect? I had walked a long distance in my dress shoes just hours before! I figured that by morning, the sensation would be gone. That was not the case.

Within a week, the burning finally did subside, but then I felt numbness in my right leg. It was nothing major, just an uncomfortable feeling when I walked. Once again, we thought it was the fault of the MG. I was not used to driving such a small sports car. This would be another reason to finally stop placating Zelda and trade her in for a less temperamental vehicle.

# CHAPTER TWO

*April 1975*

THE FOLLOWING SPRING, Don and I decided to start checking the real estate section in the Sunday papers. The lease on our apartment was up in a few months, and we were ready to buy our first home. After months of searching, we found a small two-story Cape Cod and fell in love with the quaintness of the old house. We were aware of some minor repairs that needed to be addressed, but for now, it was just what we were hoping to find.

What we thought were a few insignificant changes to the house turned into a monumental task. Little did we know the extent of the renovations that we would encounter over the next several years! As first-time home owners, the only project we envisioned was replacing the ancient monster of a furnace in the basement to make room for our state-of-the-art game room. Ironically, in the seven years that we lived in the house, we never did get around to replacing the old furnace. A sharp crack with a large wrench usually did the trick to get the old gal to run in the winter!

The first evening after we moved into our "dream home," I was replacing the old shelf paper in a kitchen cabinet and noticed a large black ant. No problem. Raid would take care of it. Less than five minutes after I sprayed, the entire kitchen floor was black with carpenter ants! Of course, I had never seen one before, so in my mind, they were giant mutant sweet ants! Now we knew where to begin our remodeling job. The fact that the previous owners left a pink range in the kitchen only added to our decision to start to renovate this room first.

It turned out that the kitchen was only the beginning of our woes. There wasn't a wall or floor in that house that did not demand our attention. We would eventually tear out every piece of carpeting, restore all the wood molding throughout the house, change the worn fixtures in the bathrooms, and replace the old weight and pulley windows with new ones.

Many nights after we stripped wallpaper, sanded floors, and tore out kitchen cabinets, we chided ourselves on the decision that we had made. We sat on the bare floors with glasses of wine and wondered if this money pit would ever be the home of our dreams.

Eventually, after a year or more of hard work and endless bank withdrawals, we were able to finish the last of the transformation. The remodeling depleted most of our meager savings, but we now had a wonderful little home of our own. We grew fruit trees in the backyard and planted a small vegetable garden with an elaborate fence that we referred to as *the llama pit*. Who knows why it ever reminded us of llamas? Don and I harvested our "crops" in the fall and, one year, even attempted to use some old mason jars that were left in the basement to preserve our dozens of pickle-sized cucumbers.

"I have a surprise for you," Don said to me one evening while we were having our dinner. He went on to explain that he had found the perfect addition to our new home, a German shepherd puppy! A man who he worked with offered Don the pick of the litter of pups that were just born to his female shepherd!

One trip to the man's farm and home we came with an eight-week old furry ball of energy. The ten-pound male came to be known as Baron the "Destructor." No matter what we did to add value to our home, in one day, Baron would destroy it.

We were naïve enough to believe that if we penned him in a small area, what harm could he do? We spent an entire weekend papering the kitchen only to come home from work one evening to a bare wall and a pile of shredded wallpaper.

Baron caused havoc with everything and everyone he came into contact with including us. He never grasped the concept of not biting the hand that fed him!

Finally, that Christmas, with a house full of family and friends, the frustrated puppy snapped at Don when he gave the dog his food. That ended the reign of terror. With no one at the house during the day, we knew it was better to find a new home for Baron.

We were lucky enough to locate a family who owned a farm with plenty of acreage for an exuberant dog to run. They had four children who were eager to have an energetic companion. Baron certainly fit the bill and would eventually weigh almost one hundred and thirty pounds as an adult. Our decision turned out to be a good one!

# CHAPTER THREE

*September 1975*

IT WASN'T LONG after the last walls were painted and the carpeting installed that I began to experience unusual headaches occurring on one side, and I noticed a blind spot in my right eye. The numb feeling in my leg that had occurred over a year ago had also returned. At this point, I thought it was time to visit a doctor.

I was referred to a well-known internist from one of the major hospitals in the Pittsburgh area. We were anxious to resolve any health issues because we wanted to start our family.

Dr. Haspen was a fiftyish gentleman with the gnarled hands of an arthritic. His handshake was warm and inviting though, and I found a sense of comfort when I explained my strange, contradictory symptoms to him. He agreed that they seemed disparate and ordered blood work as well as a referral to an ophthalmologist for the visual oddity. He did not seem concerned by the numbness in my leg and explained that until my blood work came back, he would *"put that on the back burner".*

I thought it was a fairly important clue in all this, but he was the doctor. If it turned into something consequential, it would eventually show up with further testing, so I never questioned his decision. The hematology reports returned with no alarming results. My visit to the ophthalmologist also went well.

"I don't think that your vision has changed *in the last twenty years*," she told me after a thorough eye exam. This seemed like an unusual statement, given the fact that I was only in my midtwenties, but again, I accepted her conclusions without further question. She sent her findings to Dr. Haspen.

At this point though, I felt frustrated. The symptoms still presented themselves with no apparent answers. When I met with the doctor at my follow-up appointment, he still felt that there was nothing to be concerned about.

"So far, everything that I checked through the blood work is negative," he explained to me. He still didn't see any need to follow up with the numbness in my leg.

"It isn't affecting your gait at all," was his response to my concern. As for the headaches, they were intermittent, so he again did not investigate their cause either.

"If they become more severe in the coming months," he told me, "I'll order more tests, but nothing seems out of the ordinary." He recommended that I make another appointment to see him in a year. In the meantime, he would give me a prescription for amitriptyline, which he told me would help the *"muscle spasms in my head."*

I was curious about amitriptyline. I was not familiar with the medication, so I researched it and was appalled to find that it was described as a *"sedative drug used in the treatment of depression"*! I knew what I was feeling! Nonetheless, the fact that the tests were inconclusive had convinced the doctor that these symptoms were all imagined. Dr. Haspen dismissed me because he couldn't find convincing evidence in the tests that would substantiate further examination. I never filled the prescription.

As time went on with an apparent decline in the symptoms, I began to doubt myself. Should I have these misgivings about his conclusions? Moliere, the great French dramatist, once wrote, "The mind has great influence over the body, and maladies often have their origins there." Maybe I was inventing the strange symptoms just as the doctor believed, but for what purpose? I was happily married, we had a wonderful home, and now we planned to start a family. I had no reason to jeopardize my plans with a hypothetical illness.

I knew that it was the lack of evidential results that led Dr. Haspen to conclude that I was creating these symptoms in my head. What had he based his findings on, and why had he not referred me to a neurologist if he could not find a cause?

Years later, when I thought back to my meeting with the doctor, I recalled how he questioned me about my lifestyle, what my immediate plans were, and if we intended to start our family anytime soon. At the time, I thought he was being a concerned and thorough practitioner. Now I realized, because the test results were inconclusive and my symptoms were all over the spectrum, he thought that I was a bored newlywed manufacturing these problems.

His statement at my last appointment summarized his "findings." "Go home, relax with your new husband, and maybe start thinking about a baby."

# *CHAPTER FOUR*

*September 1977*

IN TIME, MY symptoms diminished to the point that we did not concern ourselves when I would feel any unusual sensations. In September, we discovered that I was pregnant! Don and I were at the Pittsburgh airport awaiting a flight to Miami. I knew that the results of my pregnancy test were due that afternoon, so I called the obstetrician's office at eight o'clock that morning from the airport lounge and received the good news!

From Miami, we were shuttled to Marco Island. We boarded a frighteningly small, rickety puddle jumper to take us there! All I could think of during the thirty-minute flight from Miami was that if we would crash into the Atlantic Ocean, no one would ever know our joyful news! The small plane made it, however, and when we finally set down safely, the first call from the hotel room was to our parents' announcing the news.

Throughout my entire pregnancy, I never experienced a problem with numbness or headaches. I delivered a healthy eight-pound baby boy by caesarian section. Don Jr. was born on the day of the summer solstice in June 1978. No problems occurred with his birth (other than the fourteen hours of labor!), and none of the original symptoms were in evidence. Maybe Dr. Haspen had been correct after all. I was putting too much emphasis on my health for no reason. Whatever I felt before, the symptoms had completely vanished.

Parenthood was incredible, and DJ (as he was called in order to distinguish him from his father) was a joy! He learned to walk before he turned nine months old and actually has never slowed down to this day.

Whatever his father was doing around our house, DJ was right behind him with his own collection of "tools," his own lawnmower, and any other equipment that his father used, DJ had a junior-sized duplicate.

Our son's first memorable incident was on Halloween, which also happens to be Don's birthday. It was still a warm day for the very end of October and a great opportunity to clean the back yard and rake some leaves. DJ was enthralled with a small open pipe near the edge of the back lawn. Filling it with stones and leaves was his chore for the afternoon. I called him away from it twice, but he would go back as soon as I turned away. The third time that I called him, he just sat next to the pipe and smiled at me. Finally, I laid down the rake and went over to pick him up.

He appeared to be sitting on the ground, but to my great surprise, when I attempted to lift him, I discovered that he had somehow managed to get his entire leg wedged into length of the pipe!

Of course, I panicked and ran into the house to call my neighbor, hoping we could extricate him. Susan came over immediately, but neither of us could free him. At least I knew that he wasn't hurt because he was laughing when Susan gave him a piece of candy to pacify him while we attempted to dislodge his leg. When we realized after several minutes that it was hopeless, she went into the house and called Don while I stayed with my son.

"Don, this is Susan, and DJ is stuck in a pipe up to his waist!" Because he knew her as "Sue," Don could not figure out who this "Susan" was and why she was calling to tell him that his son was stuck in a pipe! Later, he would tell the story:

*"I had no idea for a minute who this woman was, and then I would hear that my son was stuck in a pipe up to his waist! For a fleeting instant, I pictured DJ caught head first in a pipe! Where is there a pipe big enough for him to be stuck from his head down to his waist? This all ran through my mind in a second's time. When Susan (I finally realized who she was) gave me more details, I comprehended that he must have somehow wedged himself into the fresh air vent on the side of the driveway."*

Susan came back out and told me that Don was on his way home. In the meantime, we had to attempt to free DJ. As silly as it may seem now, my initial thought was to call the fire company. What I thought of was the proverbial kitten in a tree! I called the police department instead who responded in a matter of minutes. My son remained calm until the two officers walked up to him with all the equipment hooked to their belts and the authoritative voices that barked orders to one another. This frightened him, and he began to cry.

"Do you have dish detergent, ma'am?" one of the officers asked me. I thought, "Oh boy, I called trained officers, and that is what they've come up with?" He thought that the soapy liquid would help dislodge DJ's shoe.

When that didn't work, the next plan was to dig around the entire area and remove the pipe from the ground with DJ's leg inside! Within the hour, the entire site around my son was excavated, and the pipe was split open to free my son's leg. Fortunately, he became so enthralled with all the shovels and tools that were being used to dig him out that he stopped crying and was thoroughly enjoying all the attention from the police. Evidently, the sole of his shoe became wedged in the "T" section at the other end of the pipe, preventing it from coming loose.

Don pulled up just in time to see a huge trench in the back yard, mounds of dirt thrown around, and a very happy little boy running over to his father as if nothing had just occurred! DJ would have quite a story to tell when he was old enough to talk!

We thanked the officers who rescued our son and then took DJ inside to assess the damage. Thankfully, he was fine with nothing more than a ruined shoe. The yard, however, was another matter. It hadn't fared as well. Don looked out the window at the carnage that was left in the yard and driveway. He laughed as he held his son and said "You know, DJ, when you are about sixteen, I am going to remind you of this!" It took Don until after eleven o'clock that evening to return the driveway to its former useable state.

# CHAPTER FIVE

IN 1980, OUR second son was born. As easy as his older brother was as a newborn, this was not the case with Sean. Because we only had two bedrooms on the first floor, both of the boys were sharing the nursery. We had cribs in opposing corners of the small room and not much else but an antique rocking chair and a combination changing table and chest of drawers.

Thankfully, DJ was a sound sleeper who wasn't awakened easily because his little brother certainly was noisy! From about ten in the evening until after four o'clock each morning, Sean cried! He was not colicky as everyone suggested, nor did he have his "days and nights" mixed up because he only had his regular sleeping pattern during the day. Sean just did not require much sleep! Unfortunately, the rest of the family did, and so I would take him out of the nursery each night, and he and I would head upstairs to the second floor.

My mother came out to help us after Sean was born. She and I would take turns inventing ways to entertain and cajole Sean so we could get a few hours' sleep. Most nights, Don would wake to find my pillow and me missing. Sometimes I would be in the living room, other times, upstairs or just shuffling around the house with my son, whispering quiet "shhh's" to him. Nothing worked! One morning, I awoke to find six empty formula bottles on the table next to the sofa where Sean and I had finally collapsed into a deep sleep. I didn't remember giving him more than the first bottle! I was beyond exhaustion!

After six weeks or more of this nightly carousel of places to sleep with Sean, he finally adjusted to a peaceful routine. I would hear him rustling around in his crib, long after he should have been sound asleep, but he was quiet, and we all felt better with a full night's rest.

With the two boys in one room, we decided that we had outgrown our little Cape Cod, and construction began on a new home, which we moved into in 1981. Our third son, Brian, was born two years later, and our family was complete.

Of the three boys, Brian was our sickest infant and eventually would be diagnosed with severe asthma. He made many trips to the emergency room for breathing treatments as a child and still battles with it today.

I remained more or less symptom-free, with none of my pregnancies contributing to my earlier problems. A few times during those years, I felt a slight numbness in my right leg but nothing severe enough for me to consult a doctor. I was puzzled when I thought of my experience with Dr. Haspen. I may have had a virus that overtook my system in those earlier years. Whatever caused the problems, would for now, remain a mystery. We were too busy with three active boys to worry about a little numbness now and then!

Don and I were having the time of our lives watching our three energetic sons learn to interact with the world around them. Swimming lessons, baseball games, and their numerous school activities kept us busy. As the parents of three children, we mastered the art of juggling our time in order to be present at all of their programs and sporting events.

Sometimes we were forced to watch two-inning baseball games, running from one field to the next, if all three of the boys played in the same evening. It was hectic but some of the most satisfying times that we shared as parents.

# CHAPTER SIX

*July 1987*

ALMOST TEN YEARS after my initial symptoms appeared, in the spring of 1987, I began to notice that by late afternoon, just about the time the boys were due home from school, I'd experience a feeling of total exhaustion. I felt so fatigued that I literally wanted to lie down on the kitchen floor. The tiredness would last until the dinner hour was over, and as suddenly as it came on, I would feel like myself again. It never crossed my mind that this lack of energy was tied to the original symptoms that I had experienced years before. Once again, I ignored the signs of anything more serious than my active routine. By midsummer, I grew accustomed to this feeling of weariness and worked my daily schedule around it.

It was time to plan our vacation, and this year, we decided to go to Bethany Beach in Delaware. We rented the greatest little house. The boys labeled it the "wooden house" because it was a one-story cedar bungalow with a dock at the end of the deck. On the "bayou" (the boys' name for the small canal running behind the house) was a small pier. We had as much enjoyment crabbing from the pier as we did spending our days on the beach. By late afternoon, the family would tire of the ocean and return to the house, shower off the day's gritty sand, and then head for the dock. The owners provided poles and crabbing nets, and each of the boys would grab something to capture his quarry.

Because Brian was still a month away from his fourth birthday, I required him to have a life vest on when he was around the water. His brothers always beat him to the crabbing gear, so he was usually left either with the broken pole or none at all. He resigned himself to walking around with the oversized net, waiting to dip it into the canal. What fun we had on those hot afternoons! We typically captured a huge pot of the "blues" each evening.

I remember the searing heat that summer. The entire east coast was in the throes of a heat wave. The temperature lingered in the midnineties for most of July and August. Along the beaches, the temperature hit the one-hundred mark most days. Evenings never cooled off much, but compared to the excessive highs during the day, the slight breezes felt comfortable. After a day on the beach, crabbing on the canal, and then dinner, we were usually exhausted by nightfall.

By midweek, we were all hoping for a quick rain shower to cool things off a bit. That never occurred, and sleeping became impossible. I decided to try the sofa in the main room, hoping it was comfortable enough to fall asleep. Although the house had window air-conditioning units, it never cooled off enough for a contented night's sleep.

As I tried to doze off one night, I felt a strange crawling sensation in my legs. It was as if thousands of spiders had been injected under my skin. It was the most bazaar feeling that I had ever experienced. The only relief that I found from this weird feeling was to place very hot towels across both of my legs.

I didn't realize at the time that I was treating the discomfort with the very heat that caused the crawling feeling in the first place!

By week's end, I was getting used to the late night ritual. During the day, I didn't feel the uncomfortable sensation. As long as I was using my legs, the motion helped to conceal the "spider effects."

We returned home from Delaware, and in a short period of time, without the presence of the high temperatures, the sensation in my legs dissipated. I never gave it another thought or questioned its implication.

# CHAPTER SEVEN

*October 1987*

THE DAILY SCHEDULES with the beginning of a new school year kept us all busy. DJ entered fourth grade in September, Sean started first grade, and Brian was beginning pre-school.

The hot autumn sun was streaming through the windshield of my car as my mother-in-law and I sat in stalled traffic. It was mid-October, and she and I were getting a jump on our holiday shopping. Brian and Pop waited for Sean to come home on the bus, and then my father-in-law was scheduled to pick up DJ from his after-school language program.

An accident was being cleared ahead, and we waited for our line of traffic to begin to move. All of a sudden, we felt a head-snapping jolt. A pick-up truck, not realizing that the cars in front of him had stopped moving, slammed into the back of our car! The impact pushed our vehicle under the rear of another truck in front of us.

It all happened so quickly that we had no time to prepare for the collision.

Fortunately, we were both wearing our seatbelts albeit years before the seatbelt law would take effect in Pennsylvania. Later, the police told us that given the rate of speed the truck was traveling, had we not been secured by the restraints, we would have definitely been injured in the crash.

The paramedics did a cursory assessment at the scene and wanted my mother-in-law to be examined at the hospital. She declined any treatment and was just anxious to get back to my house. One of the officers took us home after we had the car towed to a local garage. We were both very sore the following day but luckily avoided any injuries . . . or so I thought.

One morning, about two weeks after the accident occurred, I was getting dressed and realized that I was slowly losing sensation and coordination in my hands. I could not button my blouse. This was the first sign that I may have sustained an injury in the accident after all.

Don and I laughed together as he attempted to put my pierced earrings in my ears, until later when we realized that I was becoming less able to control my hands at all! The final indication came that afternoon as I tried to sign a school paper for Sean. I could not hold a pen, no less legibly sign my name. Had the collision caused injuries that we had not suspected until now?

I am not a pessimist by nature and also learned, as the mother of three boys, not to panic until the event was in crisis mode. There were too many scrapped knees, brotherly disagreements, haircuts at the hands of another's bad aim (Sean and his friend decided to give Brian a quick haircut one afternoon while I was sorting laundry) to be overly upset by this dilemma. I used the same justification that I did when I excused the other strange occurrences: with Zelda, with Dr. Haspen, being overcome with exhaustion last year, and more recently, the weird crawling sensations while on vacation. I would give this a few days before I sought medical treatment. Sure enough, within the following week, I regained my coordination, and the dexterity returned to normal in both of my hands.

# CHAPTER EIGHT

*October 1987*

HALLOWEEN WAS A big holiday in our house with three little goblins as well as Don's birthday. As in previous years, I stayed at home to greet the trick-or-treaters, and their father took the boys around the neighborhood to collect their "loot." Nana and Pop came to the house each year to see the boys dressed in their costumes. Pop loved to help "inventory" the candy, and then we would have a birthday celebration!

This year, I was a room mother for Sean's first-grade class. Halloween is always fun to celebrate with a class full of six- and seven-year-olds. I wore my witch costume, complete with a black hat, pointed rubber nose and chin, and my dangling spider earrings.

Something felt different though as I carted two one-gallon jugs of the drink down the hallway for the party. I had to stop several times. I thought it was probably the shoes I was wearing as part of my costume. Why else could I not make the short trip from my car to the classroom?

Since the auto accident, I was experiencing unusual sensations in my right leg and midriff. I had a tight feeling as if a band was around my midsection. The numbness in my leg had also returned. Maybe I was too quick to sign off with the insurance company concerning any injuries after the accident. First, I had the problem with my hands, and now, I was experiencing these latest sensations.

The other room mother that year happened to be a physical therapist. I described the strange symptoms to Janie and asked what she thought. I told her about the recent accident and the loss of coordination in my hands. Did she think it may be a pinched nerve somewhere in my neck or back? She listened to my list of symptoms and suggested that I call the neurologist on staff at the local hospital. "Dr. Levitt is very good," she said, "and from what you are describing, you may want to have him check things out."

It took a couple of weeks to get an appointment with the neurologist. My symptoms continued but were mild enough not to cause much discomfort. I was still convinced that I had a pinched nerve somewhere, so I had no apprehension when I arrived for my appointment. Don wanted to go with me, but it was pointless to take time off for a simple consultation.

I left Brian with my friend, Janice. She lived in our neighborhood, and Brian and her son, Josh, were good friends. I wasn't expecting the consultation to be very long. I filled in the reams of paperwork and finally was ushered in to meet Dr. Levitt. He was about my age, and we shared stories of our boys who all played little league baseball in the same area. I described my symptoms to him and told him about the recent accident and the problem that occurred with my hands. He asked me if I had ever experienced anything like this before I was involved in the accident.

"Years ago, right after I was married," I answered. "I saw a doctor for some numbness in this same leg." I told him about the blind spot as well as the headaches. He wanted to know about Dr. Haspen's findings and how he treated the conditions. I reluctantly told him about the amitriptyline and how the doctor thought I should consider having a baby!

Dr. Levitt laughed. "That was over a decade ago, and the medical community has come a long way in diagnostic testing. I would like to research his findings."

I gave him the pertinent information about the hospital where the tests had been conducted. Unfortunately, the doctor had retired, and I was not sure if another doctor would have my records.

After he finished a thorough physical examination, I asked him what he thought and if, in his opinion, the accident was the cause.

"Well, I would like to have you admitted to the hospital for a few days to conduct some tests, but to answer your question, I think it may be multiple sclerosis!"

His words burned into me like something searing the folds of my brain. Multiple sclerosis! How would Don take care of the boys if I couldn't walk? How would this change their lives? A thousand questions flooded my mind in a matter of minutes. I still held a glimmer of hope that all I had was an injury caused from the collision. The eternal optimist in me believed that the doctor had to be wrong. I would schedule the tests, and Dr. Levitt would find that the accident had caused nerve damage, maybe a disc problem, or a neck injury that had not shown up with just the physical exam. There had to be a correlation between the accident and what I was experiencing.

I knew nothing about multiple sclerosis except that it could cause paralysis. I recall reading about it in waiting room pamphlets. The statistics, then insignificant to me, now took on a whole new meaning. Three times as many females were diagnosed with MS than males of the same age. The average age for the onset of the disease was somewhere between twenty and forty. I was thirty-six! The doctor had to be wrong about me though. This was too much of a coincidence so soon after the accident.

I called Janice to let her know that I would be a bit late picking up Brian as the appointment had run longer than I anticipated. I wasn't ready to face anyone until I could wrap my mind around the doctor's conjecture. The other boys were not due back from school for a few hours, so I had time to compose myself beforehand. I drove straight home and called Don at work.

"Do you know what the doctor thinks I have?" Those were my words verbatim when Don answered his phone. "Multiple sclerosis!" My anxious voice belied any attempt to sound nonchalant. "Dr. Levitt would like me to be admitted into the hospital to run some tests!"

Don's comment came after a pause. "I was afraid of that!" he said. His statement left me speechless. What did he know that I didn't? Had he considered the crash? He and I had discussed all the possibilities and agreed that the odd symptoms had to be the result of the accident. When I finally found my voice again, I questioned his statement.

"Is there something that you are not telling me?" I asked him. "You still think this is related to the accident, don't you?"

Don hesitated before he answered. "I spoke to a few people about the type of symptoms you are exhibiting," he explained. "I researched it further, and multiple sclerosis keeps popping up as a possibility." I could tell that he was choosing his words carefully.

"We can ask Mom and Dad to come out to the house and take care of the boys. It's better that we find out for certain, right?"

The decision was made that evening, and we sat down with our sons. As best we could, given their young ages, we tried to explain what was happening and the plans that we made. DJ was old enough at nine to understand that this was not routine. I could tell by the way he watched his father's expressions that he did not fully believe the simplicity of our explanation. Sean and especially Brian had few questions. I am pretty sure that they may have stopped listening after we told them that their grandparents were going to be visiting with them for a couple of days. They knew about the accident, so we felt that this would help them to understand why I had to be away from home for a little while to have the tests performed.

# CHAPTER NINE

*November 1987*

I WAS ADMITTED to the hospital on a Tuesday morning. I hugged DJ and Sean when they left for school. I tried to reassure them both that this was the best and easiest way for the doctor to make certain that nothing happened from the accident, and that I would call each evening to talk with them.

My heart broke when I looked at their expressions. They were just little boys, and for the first time in their lives, their mother was not going to be home with them. No matter how innocuous I made this seem, they still had doubts. Brian hugged me tightly then stood next to his grandfather as we pulled out of the driveway. I turned and waved to him until he was out of sight. I am not sure as a four-year-old that he really comprehended the situation, probably expecting me to be home that evening.

If the insurance industry's guidelines were what they are today, I would have had all of my tests on an out-patient basis. However, in 1987, they were a bit more lenient about doctors' orders and what was best for the patient. Dr. Levitt ordered a myelogram, a spinal tap, CT scan, and an Evoked Response test, which checks the brain's electrical response to stimulation of the sensory system. He also ordered numerous blood cultures. He was able to research my previous records from Dr. Haspen and could compare them with his current findings. An MRI (magnetic resonance imager), although in existence since the 1970s, was not readily available in many of the smaller hospitals yet. Only approximately 300 were in operation by the end of 1986. Today, they are one of the best diagnostic tools for determining a diagnosis of multiple sclerosis. The scans conclusively show whether lesions are present on a patient's spinal cord and in the brain.

I spent the next three days in the hospital. The boys and I had a "code," and at eight o'clock each evening, I would call them from the hospital to let them know that Daddy had just left me, and now I wanted to visit with them. Don's parents told me later that it was the highlight of their day.

I was so blessed to have such loving in-laws. They would do anything for me, and during this family crisis, they were there for us without hesitation. Of course, I knew what a wonderful couple they were long before they had to demonstrate it under these circumstances. I would tease Don, telling him that I would have married him just to have his parents for my in-laws.

For the most part, the tests that were being performed were noninvasive. I didn't mind the probing and needle pricks that accompanied them. On the second day of testing, however, the technicians were preparing me for a myelogram. Dye would be injected into my spinal fluid and an x-ray taken. Because of the invasive nature and risk factors involved with this test and also with the advent of the MRI, a myelogram is used less frequently today in determining a diagnosis of multiple sclerosis.

This was the first test of this sort that I had ever experienced, so I had no frame of reference. The table that I was strapped to (and now I know why) was tipped on an angle with my head lowered to allow the dye to travel through my spinal column. With the presence of the dye in my spinal fluid, the nerve roots and cord can be examined more extensively.

The problem occurred when the mechanism jammed somehow in the downward position. The technicians were unable to right the table, so I found myself hanging from the straps that bound me. I must have remained in that position for nearly thirty minutes before they were able to finally straighten the table. The following day, I felt as if I had fallen off a cliff. Every muscle was sore, and my shoulders ached from the weight of my body's tension on the restraints. At this point, I didn't care what the test showed; I was ready to go home to my family.

The evening before my discharge, Dr. Levitt came into the hospital room as we were waiting for the papers to be processed.

"The tests are conclusive," he began. "You have a textbook case of multiple sclerosis." We were in no way surprised by the news at this point, yet hearing the doctor confirm the diagnosis felt as if I had been knocked off my feet. I looked at the aggrieved look in Don's eyes. I knew that he felt as if he had been punched in the stomach. No matter how he was dealing with this, however, I knew that he would remain strong for me. He was trying not to show the anguish that he was feeling, but I knew him too well.

Dr. Levitt continued to explain in layman's terms exactly what the test showed and what we should expect as the disease progressed. "MS is a degenerative, autoimmune disorder," he began. "This means that your body may have a reaction to a natural virus or antibody. It will attack the myelin that surrounds your spinal cord. When this happens, the myelin breaks down, and the resulting lesion forms scar tissue," he explained. "Consequently, the nerve impulse cannot reach from the brain to the affected area, causing an exacerbation . . ."

The doctor went on with his medical jargon, but by then, my mind was miles from that hospital room. I thought of our sons and the impact that this would have on them. They were so young. All of the wonderful plans that we had intended could be destroyed by this diagnosis.

"I know that this is a very hard thing to hear and has hit you both like a ton of bricks," the doctor continued. "If you have any concerns, or at anytime, questions arise, please call my office, and I will get right back to you."

Don spoke in a quiet tone. "Dr. Levitt, eighty-five percent of my life is lying in that bed. Are you absolutely sure that Bonnie's diagnosis is correct, and we should not be looking for other causes?"

Dr. Levitt looked at Don with a poignant expression and answered. "Unfortunately, yes, it is. As I said before, it is a textbook case. I would like you to think about getting a second opinion though," he told us. "There are some excellent neurologists in the city, and I can give you their names. I will in no way be offended that you are seeking another opinion." He added, "In fact, I encourage you to do so. If it was my wife, I would use every resource available to me."

After the doctor left, Don and I sat in silence. I guess we felt that if we did not confirm the reality of what we just heard that it could not be true. If we just did not acknowledge it, it wouldn't be so! We knew though that we had to pick up the pieces of our life and continue to be the family that we were before we were told this disparaging news.

As promised, Dr. Levitt gave us the names of some highly recommended neurologists in the area. We made an appointment to see one of the doctors on the list right after Thanksgiving weekend.

# CHAPTER TEN

*Thanksgiving 1987*

I WAS DISCHARGED from the hospital on the Saturday before Thanksgiving. This is one of my favorite holidays. It preceded the rush of the Christmas season and a time for our family and friends to share the abundance of food and the camaraderie of being together.

Our Thanksgiving always begins with the Macy's Day Parade airing in the background while we prepare the turkey. At eleven fifty-five, Santa rides through Times Square, and the endless hours of football take over the screen from that point on. This year would be the exception.

My mother had plans to fly in from New Jersey in a few hours to celebrate the holidays with us. We never imagined that her reservations would coincide with this cataclysmic family news.

The task fell to Don to pick her up himself. He had a small window of time to bring me back from the hospital before leaving for the airport. We did not tell my mother anything about the hospital stay or the doctor's suspicions that my symptoms were not related to the collision.

In retrospect, maybe we should have told her everything in order for her to digest it all beforehand. I saw the fractured look on her face as she walked through the door. I knew that Don must have explained everything to her on the trip home.

We embraced; our tears mingling. Don and his parents stood silently and watched as mother and daughter held one another.

In another minute, the boys clamored down the stairs to greet Nana Josie. Children have a way of realigning the world. They all ran into their grandmother's outstretched arms. It was a therapeutic moment for her. She needed normalcy after being mentally assaulted by our news. When the lighthearted conversation ran its course and her grandsons returned to their video games, Don's parents, my mother, and I sat in silence for what seemed like an eternity, although it was not even a moment. No one wanted to acknowledge the elephant in the middle of the room. Finally, my mother broke the silence.

"I knew there had to be more to it than just the accident!" she declared, smacking her hand down on the counter. "Every time I drive past the MS Support sign near my house, I turn my head!" Josie had an uncanny way of surmising things and then drawing her own conclusions. That little Italian mother of mine was one of the most superstitious people I have ever known.

I laughed for the first time in days. "Well, had we known," I said, "we could have spared the doctor a lot of time trying to figure this all out!" This broke the tension in the room, and for a short period of time, our family was unconcerned about what the future held for us.

Much to my chagrin, it was decided that we would enjoy this Thanksgiving dinner at a restaurant. Because I am a traditionalist when it comes to the holidays. I follow the same routine each year and for every holiday. Try as I might to convince everyone that I was fine, I was outvoted, and we made reservations to dine out.

My family was more than supportive. I understood their anxiety and how much they all cared about my well-being. However, after just the small decision regarding our Thanksgiving meal, I realized that I was going to have to battle my way back to the sovereignty I had before the diagnosis. I felt that I was already becoming invisible. Other than the slight numbness and tingling in my hands and legs, I had no other signs of MS. I continued to do all that I did before, and honestly, I was relieved to at least have a definitive cause now. After all the years of thinking that I was inventing these strange conditions, at least now I knew the reason for them and would adjust my life accordingly.

# CHAPTER ELEVEN

THE FOLLOWING TUESDAY, we walked INTO the Pittsburgh Neurological Associates for our ten o'clock appointment. We had chosen a doctor for the second opinion who came highly recommended for his work with MS patients. His name was Benjamin Lancoses, and he was considered one of the city's top specialists in his field.

We were ushered into his office and introduced to the doctor. He was in his late forties according to his bio online but appeared older. He wore wire-rimmed glasses that were perched on his forehead. He invited us to sit while he read over my medical information. Several minutes went by with no one speaking. Finally, about the time I began to feel uncomfortable with the silence, Dr. Lancoses looked up. He had a stunned look on his face almost as if he was surprised by our presence. OK, I am a bit of a cynic, and this did not give me a warm fuzzy feeling.

"In reading her chart and Dr. Levitt's findings," he began. "I see no reason to even examine her today as this is a clear cut case of multiple sclerosis." He was addressing Don as if I was not even in the room with them! "I deal with many patients with this profile, and it is what it is."

I was almost waiting for him to exclaim, "Period!"

Without any acknowledgement from us, he continued. "My suggestion is to prepare for an eventual time when this disease will take a more aggressive turn." The entire time that he spoke to us, he continued to address Don, referring to me in the third person!

He took his glasses off, leaned back in his office chair, and proceeded to clean them over his head with a tissue he had taken from a box on the desk. Now he was speaking to the ceiling as he checked for smudges that he may have missed on his lenses.

I guess because I was still reeling from the diagnosis and hoping that we were going to hear more positive news from a second opinion, this doctor's arrogant, dismissive demeanor did not irritate me as it would have under different circumstances.

"My recommendation is to move to a one-story house if possible, have the doors widened so an eventual wheelchair will fit . . ."

At this point, I heard enough! I gathered up the sheet of questions I had planned to ask and put them in my purse. I glanced at Don and as if he read my signal, stood, and extended his hand.

"Thank you for seeing us Doctor and reviewing my wife's chart (amazing that my name had still not been spoken). You have answered our key question, as to whether this is definitively MS."

With that, we all shook hands and left his office.

# CHAPTER TWELVE

*December 1987*

WE ALL SETTLED into a cautious but comfortable routine as we prepared for the upcoming Christmas season. The boys returned to school after Thanksgiving break, although at this time of year, I am not sure how much actual learning took place. Talk of Christmas parties, the latest and best toys, and holiday projects took precedence.

I threw myself into researching MS with a desire to learn everything I could about this disease. My mother was coming to terms with it in her own way, and I let her ask her questions as they arose. I tried to put her mind at ease by answering them in the most benign way. Don and I felt optimistic after a second meeting with Dr. Levitt. I physically felt great, so I was not sure why everyone was so anxious about my prognosis. Through my exploration into what triggered an exacerbation, I mentally charted a pattern of moving forward with my life. I felt in complete control and would deal with whatever happened.

My confidence was short-lived. Less than two weeks after Thanksgiving, my leg collapsed while I was folding laundry. As quickly as it buckled, however, I was able to stand on it again. My first thought was that I had turned quickly and twisted my knee, but I recalled the doctor's advice to me when I left the hospital. "If any suspicious or unexplainable happens," he told me, "I want you to call my office immediately."

I was able to reach him directly and told him what had just occurred. "Chances are good that it will be nothing," Dr. Levitt told me on the phone, "but I'd like to see you this afternoon if at all possible."

When I walked into his office less than an hour later, the receptionist immediately called the nurse who brought me back to the exam room. The doctor was waiting for me. I was becoming a bit more concerned now. What seemed to me to be a very minor incident was being treated as a major event!

"Explain to me exactly what happened when your knee collapsed," Dr. Levitt asked.

I told him that I was standing by the table folding some laundry and had not even taken a step when it happened. He examined my leg by first observing me walk across the room and then checking the strength by having me push against his hand then pull back again. He finished the exam and told me what he thought had occurred.

"What you experienced today was definitely MS-related," he began. "In simple terms, the nerve that sends an impulse from your brain to your leg short-circuited for a second or two. Had you been sitting down when this happened," he explained, "you would not have even been aware of anything taking place."

"Welcome to Multiple Sclerosis 101," I said to him with a small laugh, but the smile never went further than my lips. His next statement terrified me. He told me that this may never happen again or may continue depending on the extent of the plaque on my spinal cord. It was a warning and something for me to be aware of in the event that I might be walking somewhere. "If it continues to happen," he suggested, "you may want to consider keeping a cane nearby for safety's sake."

The doctor said this in a matter-of-fact way but now my heart dropped to my feet! A cane! Up until this point, I thought of the disease as an inconvenience to deal with now and then. I hadn't bargained for something like this to happen or the ramifications of it.

As I walked from his office that afternoon, the consequences of MS finally set in. It was my "aha" moment. Everyone closest to me had already realized what I obviously had not fully accepted yet. I thought my husband and my mother overreacted when they heard the diagnosis. I pooh-poohed their concerns. The crippling effects of multiple sclerosis could happen to others maybe but surely not to me. I was in denial . . . until now!

I pulled out of the parking lot and turned toward home. How could I feel fine and then have this hit me so suddenly? I read everything that *could* happen, but I obviously had not prepared myself for the fact that it may happen so unexpectedly. Well, I was not going to wallow in self-pity and throw in the towel. I could handle this little crisis.

Following the traffic, I mentally prepared myself to convey this latest setback to the family. Until now, we were able to simplify anything that had to do with MS where the boys were concerned. I didn't want to frighten them. They asked me after I was first diagnosed in the fall if they could "catch" the disease. I tried to explain to them that they probably meant "if they could inherit the disease" and went on to explain *that* to them. We told them what the future may hold, and we agreed that we would make all of our decisions as a family. Don and I asked the boys to promise that if they had any questions or concerns, to please talk to us about them – don't keep anything that bothered them to themselves. He and I also made a pact with one another. Any decision that we made would not be based on this illness. We would move forward and continue making our family choices as we would have had I never been diagnosed. MS would never interrupt our lives.

Now here I was with the first visible crisis. A cane was an overt sign that something was wrong. Was I prepared mentally for others to see me as a handicapped person? All my life I had treasured my independence. I prided myself on two things, my autonomy and my privacy. Now I may be forced to relinquish both and ask for assistance. I may have to depend on others to help me to live my life. I couldn't do it!

## CHAPTER THIRTEEN

I WAS NEARING the house. As I prepared to turn the corner into my street, I tried to step on the brake to slow down and realized that I could not move my right leg! I could not lift it from the accelerator to the brake. It was dead weight! I manually lifted it off of the gas pedal and pulled to the side of the road. I sat there in a daze. What was happening? Again, I tried to move my leg, but it reacted as if it was no longer part of my body.

After ten minutes, I knew that I had to do something. I was a block from the house, and I had to get there somehow. Using my left foot on the brake, I lifted my right foot and placed it back on the accelerator. I put the car in gear and slowly crept up the hill toward my address. By controlling the speed of the car with my left foot, I pulled into the driveway and turned off the engine.

Until this day, I cannot recall how I managed to get from the car into the house. It is a blur. The next memory I have is calling the doctor's office and explaining to him what had just happened.

"I need you to meet me in the emergency room," he said. "I am going to admit you and begin treatment, so you will want to make arrangements for your family."

# MY STORY

By this point, my mind was spinning. Everything was happening too quickly. I had planned to call Don to tell him what had transpired earlier in the day. Now I was calling to ask him to take me to the hospital because I couldn't walk. I waited for him to pick up his office phone.

"Hi," I whispered. Then there was only dead air.

"Bon?" he questioned. "Are you there?" I finally found my voice.

"I need you to come home," I told him in a flat tone. I had to keep the alarm out of my voice.

His voice rose. "What happened? Are the boys all right?"

I took a deep breath and told him all the events that had occurred: my leg buckling, seeing the doctor, then my leg collapsing on the drive home from the doctor's office just now and my current situation.

"I can't use my right leg. I can't walk!" I cried. "I called the doctor, and he is meeting us in the emergency room as soon as we can get there."

"I'm leaving now." Don disconnected the call.

We drove to the hospital in silence. All our uncertainty and the questions we'd been asking about the course of the disease now crashed down on us, and we had none of the answers. I knew what I was sensing at this moment, so I could only imagine the dread that Don was feeling.

I wanted to tell him that everything would be all right; I needed to calm his fears. Wasn't I the one who, for all our married life, found the silver lining in his clouds? I literally could not speak.

I could not form a sentence. Absolute dread had taken over my whole being.

Don reached over and took my hand. "We'll get through this," he said, breaking the silence. "Let's give Dr. Levitt a chance to check you out and start this treatment that he told you about."

All I could do was nod.

# *CHAPTER FOURTEEN*

A YOUNG HISPANIC attendant came out of the emergency room door with a wheelchair and took me into the hospital. This was the beginning of a long journey. I had two options. I could either let others take care of me, or I could fight this disease with every ounce of strength and courage that I could gather.

I knew that there was no choice to be made. I had three little boys at home who needed their mother. I also had an incredible husband, and I was not going to let MS devour me and destroy my family! I would not place them on the sidelines because I was thrown a curve. We would get through this as a family, and the mission must begin with me.

The aide took me into the examination room where Dr. Levitt awaited us. He had already made arrangements for my stay in the hospital and asked Don to approve this with the admissions office.

"While we are waiting for Don to return," the doctor began, "I'm sure that you are reeling at this point because you never had a chance to digest what happened earlier this afternoon when you came to my office. Unfortunately," he continued, "that was a precursor to what is happening now. Whatever triggered this exacerbation has to run its course."

I had so many questions, but I wanted Don to be present as I knew he had many of his own. He walked in a moment later. As if Dr. Levitt read our minds, he said, "I know how many questions you both must have, and I will answer them all for you, but first, let me explain the treatment. As I told you when we last met, each case of MS exhibits different symptoms, and therefore, we treat each case accordingly."

Don walked over to my side and took my hand.

"I am going to begin a treatment of intravenous steroids called ACTH, short for adrenocorticotrophic hormone, which is a powerful hormone. It is extracted from the beef pituitary gland and used to stimulate the cortisone output by the human adrenal gland." He must have seen our puzzled look. "In simple terms," he said, "it will help your body stop its self-destruction."

"The longer you remain out of remission and don't use the affected area, your leg in this case, the more probable it is that your brain will no longer respond to the nerve stimulus. The faster we get you to move that leg, the better chance you will have for a full recovery."

This information prompted me to interrupt the doctor. "So what is the best means of accomplishing this in the shortest amount of time? Will the ACTH act fast enough?" I asked him.

"I am setting you up with our physical/occupational therapy department as well. You will have a morning and afternoon session each day. I can't stress enough how important the therapy is in your recovery," he told me. "I've explained about the myelin breaking down when you have an attack. This is the demyelization, but it can be reversed."

This gave me a small ray of hope. He continued to explain that the gel coating surrounding the spinal cord, the myelin, can repair itself.

"This is why it is so important to keep the nerve stimuli flowing between the brain and the affected area. Physical therapy will help to do this."

Dr. Levitt stayed with us to answer our many questions. Christmas was three weeks away, but the doctor could give us no definitive response to our questions about time. How long before I could go home to my family? How long before the drug will begin to show evidence of a change in my symptoms? Would intense therapy speed the process? Would I be able to celebrate Christmas at home?

On and on we pummeled the doctor with questions like these. It was unfair to expect clear cut answers to our inquiries though. We knew that he had barely assessed the amount of damage yet or had time to run any tests. I had not been evaluated by the physical therapy unit either. All we could do tonight is comfort one another and figure out how we would get through the next several weeks.

When Dr. Levitt finally left, I looked at Don without speaking. I saw the pained expression and such deep concern in his eyes. I had to make him believe in me and know how hard I was going to fight to regain the use of my leg. I drew a deep breath and said, "We can do this . . . together. I can do all that they tell me to do in therapy, but I need you to be there for the boys."

All he could do in response was to reach over and hug me.

## CHAPTER FIFTEEN

EXCEPT FOR A few hours near dawn, I spent a sleepless first night in the hospital. The nurses and lab set me up with the intravenous medication. I received my first dose of the ACTH that evening and continued with it twice daily for the next three weeks. I was scheduled to be evaluated in the morning by the physical therapy team.

Throughout all the activity of these initial preparations, I could not turn off my mind. The fact that I was here was bad but because it was so close to the holidays, the timing could not have been worse. It made the entire experience even more agonizing.

I pictured the boys' faces and wondered what they thought when their grandmother and father told them where I was and what had happened. Of course, I called them so they could hear my voice and to promise them that I was all right. I tried to make light of the circumstances.

"I am going to ask Santa to fix my leg," I told Brian. He assured me that he was going to put that on his list! I tried to reassure them as best I could, but a voice over the phone and soothing words would never replace a hug when their world has been turned upside down.

DJ was a worrier by nature. I knew that he was as upset as everyone else, but he would internalize his feelings for the sake of his two younger brothers. He would never let them see that he was feeling as confused and anxious as they felt. He was his father's son and would try to appear as strong and diligent as his first-born nature would allow.

I was blessed to have Don's parents and my mother with them. It not only helped to assuage the feelings of helplessness that I was experiencing but also for their father to know that our children were with those who cared for them as much as we did as their parents. Don wanted to be there for his sons, their grandparents, and for me as well. He was being pulled in so many directions.

Word spread quickly to all our friends and neighbors. I can never repay the kindness that was shown to our family during those next awful months. Food was brought to the house on a daily basis.

At one point, my mother called me to say that she had no more room for the pans of lasagna in the freezer!

I spoke to the boys and my mother by phone each day. I knew it was the only connection that they had with me. It also helped me to focus on my therapy. I hung on to each of the doctor's words. I recalled watching a program one evening about ALS (amyotrophic lateral sclerosis or Lou Gehrig's disease). When I witnessed the devastating results of the disease, all I could focus on was the word "sclerosis"! I was in a panic until Dr. Levitt assured me that I did not have that type of sclerosis and was not dealing with anything remotely close to it.

As the days wore on, I began to follow a schedule; the medication dripped into my arm each morning, then onto physical therapy. It was determined that I would receive therapy once in the morning and then again after lunch. Don somehow found the time to shop for several "designer" exercise outfits for me. I felt like a handicap fashion model when I would roll into the therapy department. Tucked away in the back of my drawer is a shirt that I saved from those sessions. It is a bittersweet reminder of where I was at that point in my life and how far I have come since then.

I was also so resolute about my recovery that I would awaken during the night and perform the various leg exercises from that day's therapy. I remember a chilling incident one morning toward the end of my first week in the hospital. The nurses helped me to move as much as possible so I spent little time in bed during the day. Usually after my morning meds were finished, they would help me into the bathroom to bath and dress. This particular morning, I was propped against the sink brushing my teeth, and when I attempted to expectorate, I couldn't do it! I could not spit out my toothpaste! My first thought was that if I could not work the muscles that controlled my mouth and tongue to achieve this simple task, would I be able to form words? Will my speech be altered as well now?

For a moment, I panicked. The nurse was just outside the bathroom door, and I motioned to her. What was happening? Instead of regaining some mobility, I was getting worse! I recalled the morning that my leg buckled and what came hours later. Was this another precursor of what may happen? First, my leg failed, and now my speech!

I read in my recent research of MS that an interruption in pronunciation or the rhythm of one's speech is called *dysarthria*. It is usually associated with slurred speech, not exactly what I was experiencing or was it?

As the nurse helped me back into bed, I explained to her what just happened to me. Was I slurring my speech when I spoke? I didn't think so and neither did the nurse. She assured me that she would make a note of it on my chart and also make the therapists aware of it. I listened for any limitations in my speech pattern or a sign that my voice had changed in any way.

During the rest of the day and evening, I spoke whenever possible and then grilled the person on the sound of my voice. No one heard me slur my speech or talk in a way that would warrant concern. When the doctor made his rounds that evening, I told him what had occurred. I pressed him on the possibility that this was mimicking the events that took place when my leg collapsed.

"It may be an isolated incident," he told me. He did not hear anything unusual when I spoke that would concern him, but he said that he would follow up with the therapists and have them evaluate me in the morning.

When I awoke the following day, the first thing I did was say something out loud. I sounded normal to my own ears, and when the nurse came in to take my vitals, I asked her to listen to me speak.

The occupational therapist performed various speech tests that day and concluded that the doctor was correct in thinking it was a onetime occurrence. "Chances are that it will never happen a second time," she said in an effort to assure me. Time proved her correct with this latest ordeal. I never experienced that sensation again.

## *CHAPTER SIXTEEN*

I CONTINUED MY meds and therapy through the weekend and into the beginning of my second week. On Monday, I was wheeled back into my room after my morning therapy session to find a smartly dressed young woman waiting to speak with me. She identified herself as Meg Stern from the Harmarville Rehabilitation Center. She held several folders and waited at the foot of my bed while the nurse helped me to settle against the pillows. Ms. Stern got right to the point.

"I have been made aware of your situation from the physical therapy department as well as the medical staff here at the hospital," she began. "We have a room reserved for you at the rehab center. We also have confirmed this with your insurance carrier and have preauthorization for your transport as well as your stay with us," she told me with a superior air of confidence.

I waited for her to take a breath, but she seemed intent on getting as much of this information out to me before I could interrupt. I allowed her to continue.

"We will equip your vehicle with hand controls . . ."

She began to pull papers from her folder as she said this. "Now, if you will sign these consent forms, we can initiate the transfer."

"I'm not going," I declared. Ms. Stern was rendered speechless for the first time since she stated her pronouncement. When she finally found her voice, she explained to me in an incredulous tone that everything was set up and that the rehab center was expecting me.

"Ms. Stern," I explained to her, "I have not seen my family in over ten days. I have almost two more weeks to continue my meds and therapy. I am then going home to my children and celebrate the holidays with them."

As she sputtered about her next course of action, I simply smiled and said that I was truly sorry if this inconvenienced her or skewed her plans in any way. The woman gathered her paperwork and folders, forced a "get well" wish through her lips, and left the room.

Nothing more transpired over the course of the next few days, and I never heard another word about the Harmarville Rehabilitation Center, hand controls, or being trained to live my life as an invalid. I wonder now, how many individuals are in wheelchairs because they had given in to the overambitious Meg Sterns of the world? Because their wide-range outlook was at its lowest point, they grasped at any type of solace and support that was being offered to them, even in the guise of a wheelchair. They hoped that this may help them to cope with their disability. I am sure that if I had gone through with her recommendations, I would have believed myself incapable of ever walking unaided again. I would have resigned myself to live as a handicapped person.

# *CHAPTER SEVENTEEN*

I KEPT IN constant contact with the boys. I was thrilled when Don walked in one evening with a present from them. It was a picture of all three sitting on Santa's lap!

I laughed until I was in tears as their father described the conspiratorial cajoling he used with DJ. He needed a non-believing nine-year-old to sit on Santa's lap with his little brothers. I cannot put into words how it felt to look at their delighted expressions in the photo. I knew they missed me as much as I did them and how excited they were to create this for me.

Of course, I called them a moment after I viewed it. I could picture them all hovering around the phone waiting to hear my reaction! They assured me that they were not having Christmas until I came home, and no one was opening any presents! I laughed through my tears.

I missed my three little guys so much. I waited for the day that I would be released from here and be able to take care of my family again. There were times when self-pity took over, and I would get in a "woe is me" funk. It never lasted long, however, because I had to keep myself on top of this disease, and my mental attitude was half the battle.

Many nights when sleep would not come, I continued to do that day's therapy to strengthen my leg. I felt so empowered by this. Does that sound crazy? I needed to know that I was fighting with all my strength. I knew that I could triumph over the worst of this disease!

Buddha's teaching believes, "All that we are is a result of what we have thought. The mind is everything. What we think, we become." I believe that when things go wrong in one's life, the mind compensates by strengthening its own convictions.

In order to fight this disease, I had to first forgive my body. We had to work together – the mind and body as one. I needed to accept this premise in order to conquer this demon within me. I could not hate it. I had to embrace it. What was the worst imaginable consequence? That someday, I would sit in a wheelchair and read to my grandchildren? If I could accept that, then I could move past it. This credence helped me to overcome the dread that I experienced in those quiet lonely nights in the hospital.

I continued to have faith in more than the tangibles provided by the doctors, therapists, and the drugs. Throughout that first week in the hospital, I did a great deal of bargaining with God. I was not sure how all this was going to turn out, but I had to believe that He was on my side.

I made a deal with myself and Him that by Easter Sunday, I would walk to the altar and receive communion in dress shoes. I intended to keep my end of the bargain, and a little help from above would surely be appreciated.

An important part of the therapy for multiple sclerosis is mental strength and the ability to remain positive. To give into the disease is to give up on one's self. I believed that I had to keep pushing the limits. I needed to be bold in my therapy as well as trust that the future would mold itself around this new person I'd become. I was no longer the individual who had entered this hospital almost a month before. I'd learned much about myself in the journey so far and would take this with me as I move forward in life. George Bernard Shaw once wrote, "What lies behind us and what lies before us are small matters compared to what lies within us."

How I relate to others now and what I think of myself are much more important than I had ever thought in the past. I have a greater appreciation for the daily management of my time. I no longer take small things for granted. The slightest accomplishment now holds greater significance for me.

My therapy team worked with me daily, and each of them treated this disability as a transitory medical condition. Not once did any of them assume that I would not gain full control and use of my leg and be able to walk again.

I wanted to maintain that strength for Don too. He needed to believe that we could beat this together. He surely was doing his part. I felt that I owed him as much.

# CHAPTER EIGHTEEN

*Mid-December 1987*

CHRISTMAS WAS FAST approaching, and the school's holiday activities were in full swing. Janie, the other room mother for our first-graders as well as one of my therapists, was wheeling me back to the room.

"I wanted to ask you if you would like to have an afternoon out. I checked with Dr. Levitt, and if you feel up to it, he is allowing me to take you to the boys' Christmas party at school."

I was speechless, and needless to say, jumped at the idea! This was my chance to see DJ and Sean, and for the first time since this happened to me, I would feel a sense of normalcy.

Everything was arranged for me to leave the hospital that Friday afternoon. Don was the only one aware of the plan. Think of the surprise for Sean when I "walked" into his classroom!

By now, I was able to use a walker. I had "foot drop" on my right side, which is a tendency for my ankle to be weak and not support my foot. Therefore, I was fitted with a brace that slipped into my shoe to help lift my foot when I walked.

On our way to the elementary school, I was in for another surprise. We took a small detour as Janie drove me to my house for just a moment to see my mother and Brian!

She pulled into the driveway and helped me to navigate the walk. I will never forget the expression on my mother's face when she opened the door and saw me standing there. She told me later that the sun shone on me in such a way that for a moment, it formed a halo above me. I knew that she was doing her best to remain on top of the situation with the house and the boys, but when she would say these things to me, I knew that she was fighting her own demons.

I hugged her tightly. We explained about our plans to surprise Sean at his party and that I did not even have time to come in for a short visit. It felt so good to be encircled in my mother's arms. For just a moment, I was five years old again and in need of a parent's comforting embrace.

Brian was behind his grandmother in the doorway, hopping from one foot to the other. He was ecstatic when he saw me. I so wanted to walk through that door and never leave. I felt like Alice when she said in the classic Lewis Carroll tale, "But it's no use going back to yesterday, because I was a different person then."

We reached the school, and Janie helped me to the classroom at the other end of the hallway. I stuck my head into DJ's class on the way. He did a double take when he saw me. I was the last person that he ever expected to be poking her head in the doorway. He came out to see me for a few minutes, and I told him why I was there. I promised him that I would do my best to be home with him for Christmas. That seemed to be my mantra whenever I spoke with the boys.

Sean was thrilled when I came into his room. His teacher knew to expect us so she made sure that he was closest to the door and saw me immediately. Needless to say, he could not believe that I actually made it to his party! He didn't expect this surprise, and after giving me a huge hug, he never left my side. We had a grand time that afternoon. What an enjoyable holiday party it was with fourteen first-graders who still believed in the wonderment of Santa! Again, as I left, I promised Sean that I would do everything possible to be home with him for Christmas.

Back in the hospital, I was more exhausted than I would have thought, but it was an exhilarating tiredness, if that is not too much of an oxymoron.

# CHAPTER NINETEEN

THIS WAS THE third week of my therapy and intravenous ACTH. I couldn't say that I saw much improvement yet, but mentally, I had turned the corner. I knew that nothing was going to prevent me from gaining my full strength. Barring something going terribly wrong between now and next Friday, I planned to be home to celebrate Christmas with my family.

On Tuesday morning, Dr. Levitt stopped in my room. He did a cursory evaluation and then pulled up a chair and sat by the foot of the bed.

"How would you like to go home in a day or so? Christmas Eve is Thursday, and I think it would help you tremendously in your recovery if you could be home with your family."

I was not expecting this and laid there wordless. Tears formed as I looked at the doctor in disbelief. I worked so hard for the last three weeks and waited patiently for him to release me. Now the moment had finally arrived.

On December 24, Christmas Eve, I was released from the hospital. This is the day that I had prayed for, and it was here at last. The shunt that dispensed the medicine into my arm was removed, and I was given my "walking papers"! Everything was packed and ready by midmorning. My last inpatient PT session was earlier in the day. The plan was to have me come in two days a week on an outpatient basis once I was released. Don was waiting in the room when I returned from therapy and had already taken all my belongings to the car.

"Are you ready?" he asked with a Cheshire grin. He was obviously as happy as I to get me home without delay. I didn't know what my mother and he had told the boys, or if they said anything at all. Obviously, if they expected me and then the discharge fell through for some reason, they would be devastated.

What a difference the drive home was for me compared to three weeks before when I left for the hospital. I had butterflies now, but they were of the good sort. In fifteen minutes, I would be home in the safety of my house and surrounded by my family. My dream of spending the holidays with them had come true.

We pulled into the driveway, and I asked Don to stop. I wanted to take in all of the wonderful sights. I looked at the wreathes hanging in the windows, the lights that even in broad daylight burned so brightly, and the best sight was the tree that glowed in the front window. Christmas was all around me. I had the most amazing family, and the sights and sounds of the holidays were the best therapy that I could have right now.

Don held my walker while I balanced myself and prepared to negotiate the front walk to the house. My mother stood in the opened door with her arms spread wide to gather me close. As we hugged, I looked past her. I was stunned by the tremendous display of poinsettias that filled the foyer. They flowed into the living room and den. She told me how overwhelmed she was by the wonderful outpouring of kindness that all of our friends and neighbors had shown to her while I was in the hospital. "Each day, they would be at the door with a poinsettia and another pan of lasagna!" she said to me.

As we talked, I realized that something was amiss. Wait . . . where were the boys? Surely they would be on pins and needles awaiting my homecoming now that my discharge was secured. There was not a sound, and before I could ask, Don saw the puzzled look on my face. He realized immediately what I was questioning. With the hubbub and rushing about to bring me home, it completely slipped his mind to tell me about the plan. A friend of ours had taken the three boys to the movies so when they returned, I would be there to surprise them.

Just then, we heard the car doors slam and knew they were home. I seated myself on the foyer steps in order for them to see me as soon as the door swung open. Even before all three were inside, they spotted me!

It was a Kodak moment and a Norman Rockwell scene brought together. To see the looks on those little boys' faces was truly a priceless moment to behold. There are no words to describe the sheer delight that I witnessed when they came through that door.

I could not help but shed tears of joy when I saw my three children. They would normally have teased me as I cry at the silliest things, but when I looked at them, they knew that these tears were from pure delight. My sons all swarmed around me and would not stop hugging me. When things quieted down enough to be heard, I said, "Needless to say, your dad pulled off quite a surprise, huh?"

The first words out of Brian's mouth were "Now we can open all the presents, DJ!" I laughed and knew we were back to normal.

We were complete. I was home with the ones I loved most in this world.

I sat in the family room flanked by all three and explained about the walker.

"There are times that I will need you boys to help me," I said to them. "You will be my legs until I can walk by myself again." I asked them to be patient with me for a while because I would need them to do errands around the house. Until I was able to walk on my own again, they had to accept my limitations.

Brian was already trying to do somersaults on the walker, and that was fine. I did not want them to feel apprehension toward any of the rehabilitation equipment that I may have to use in the coming months. After a head-first tumble onto the floor, however, the walker lost its significance and was no longer a novelty.

# CHAPTER TWENTY

## Christmas Morning

EVER SINCE THE boys were old enough to run down the hall on Christmas morning, the tradition was always the same. They had to pass their grandmother's room in order to get to our bedroom door. It was my mother's job to intercept them before they made it all the way down the hallway to our room. They would all crawl into her bed until she gave them the okay to awaken us.

Her stock line to them was, "Wait until your father has his cup of coffee!" Of course, that never happened because as soon as they heard us in the hallway, they would run out of her room and bound down the stairs.

Each year, long before anyone awoke, I would sneak down to start the coffee and make sure the tree lights were lit and the cookies were removed from under the tree. Santa's note had to be left in the empty plate as well.

This year would prove to be a much different holiday in many ways. I needed help to descend the stairs and found that the easiest and safest way was to sit and slide down on my backside. I tried to stifle my laughter because it was only a quarter to five in the morning. I had to awaken Don so he could carry the walker down for me. I also needed his help to get everything ready. Being Santa's helper on one leg can be a heady experience.

I sent Don back upstairs, and an hour later, I heard the commotion coming from Nana's room. They soon found out that I was already downstairs and came crashing into the family room. The tree was glowing, and the packages were all around the tree. I was sitting near the doorway, waiting for the onslaught!

I knew I was responsible for the tone of the holiday this year. In the past, I was the conspirator who planned the surprises, the music director who kept the carols playing, the organizer of the menus throughout the days of Christmas, and lastly, the mother who baked the cookies, glued the head back onto He-Man, found the missing puzzle piece, and pacified the ill-tempered sibling who didn't like the name his brother had called him. Christmas would be no different this year, and I was determined that it was going to be as happily unforgettable as our past holidays.

When all the presents were unwrapped and the boys were busy showing Nana Josie how their latest electronic gadgets worked, Don and I quietly slipped from the room and sat on the steps in the hallway.

We held one another and cried. We shed tears for the current circumstances but more, I think, in relief for the way things turned out. It was the satisfaction and contentment of knowing we had pulled off the last month somehow and came through it with little collateral damage to our family. We had fashioned a Christmas that the boys would remember as a joyful one.

Don and I had no answers as to what was going to ultimately happen with me down the road. How many concessions and adjustments were we going to make? Was this the beginning of a different lifestyle for our children?

We were not going to dwell on those questions today. Christmas was a time for celebration and family unity. Don's parents were due in a few hours, and there was dinner to prepare, wrapping paper and ribbon to clean up, and a host of busy chores as our holiday continued to unfold.

The remainder of the day and evening flew by. My in-laws came in with another armload of gifts. More presents were opened, our dinner was wonderful, and with all the desserts that our friends and neighbors brought to the house while I was in the hospital, we would enjoy them for days to come.

Don's parents left about eight o'clock that evening, and by then I was exhausted. It had been a heartwarming homecoming for me, and today's festivities went by without a glitch.

# CHAPTER TWENTY-ONE

WE WERE ROUNDING up the boys and their gifts when DJ walked into the living room crying! Don and I looked at one another in bewilderment as we followed him into the living room.

"What's the matter, honey?" we asked him. My first thought was that he had not received a gift for Christmas that he had asked for. At nine, that can be a disappointing thing.

By now he was crying hard, and we were both sitting there with our arms around him, trying to determine what had happened.

Finally, he had calmed down enough to tell us what was wrong.

"The day that you came to Sean's party, someone in my class called you a cripple!" he told me, still crying. I realized that this strong little boy of ours had kept this terrible hurtful remark to himself for the last ten days and never said a word to anyone.

"DJ, why didn't you tell us about this after it happened? I asked him.

He responded, "I didn't want to ruin Christmas for anyone."

"Oh honey, I am so sorry, I never thought when I came to the school using a walker that anyone would say something like that."

My heart was broken. With all my good intentions, I had instead caused my son great pain.

"This person was wrong, DJ, not only for saying such a cruel thing to you but also because I am not a cripple. In a few months, I will be walking again."

He quieted down, and I asked him to believe that before long, I would be back to normal. I knew how difficult this was for him. Being the oldest, he was most aware of what was happening. This gave me even greater resolve to walk again!

# CHAPTER TWENTY-TWO

*January 1988*

THE HOLIDAY SEASON was over. I was so appreciative to everyone who made it special. I was most blessed to have Don in my life. He stood beside me throughout all the difficult times and comforted me in my darkest moments. There was nothing that I would ask of him that he wouldn't do for me. Our sons took their father's lead and helped with any of the added responsibilities with never a complaint.

Don took on the chore of the weekly grocery shopping. He would take the two older boys with him. They were both old enough to know better but young enough to still cause sheer havoc through the aisles. To this day, when Don sees the infamous display of large balls in the front of a grocery store, he cringes! More than once, he's chased one down an aisle. He never knew when a sponge would fly over the top of one aisle into the next, but at least he knew where the boys were located. Once, an older woman "scolded" him for not having more control over his children!

I enjoyed emptying the bags after they returned because there were always surprise items that were not on the list but found their way into the cart. I was never sure whether the boys were sneaking them in or Don just wanted to get through the store as fast as possible and grabbed anything that looked edible!

My mother changed her return reservations and took over the day-to-day household chores. I had so many neighbors and friends who offered their assistance with driving, meals, and the boys' school schedules. Several of my friends even created a carpool calendar between them to drive me to my therapy sessions twice a week. Without that support, I am not sure how we would have managed with all that had to be tended to. It was such a break for Don to know that schedules were kept while he went to work each day.

I slowly gained more strength in my leg. I tried to do as much on my own as possible. One afternoon, I decided to make myself a cup of tea. While my mother was busy with the boys, I used my walker to navigate into the kitchen. With perseverance, I moved from the cupboard with my cup to the canister for my teabag. I moved the walker a few more feet, and I filled the cup with water and placed it in the microwave. After it brewed and I was ready for the return trip, I had to devise a route so that I could place the hot tea on reachable surfaces, move myself on the walker, and then move my cup again until I was back in the family room.

I felt such a sense of accomplishment. When I sat down with my freshly brewed cup of tea, my mother (still stunned at what I had just done) came over to my chair and said, "I have been trying to knock that independence out of you since you were a little girl. I'm glad now that I didn't!"

# CHAPTER TWENTY-THREE

THE FIRST TIME away from the security of my home and family was a community event after the holidays. The annual pancake breakfast was held as a fund-raiser for the boys' baseball league, and I decided that this would be a great opportunity to "try out my wings." I would be among old friends, some who hadn't seen me since I entered the hospital. It would feel good to be surrounded by them and talk about something more than my disability. I had forgotten the ordinary life that I took for granted just months before.

My happy expectations were brief, though. I noticed that the same people, who six weeks ago talked to me in the off-handed tone of an old friend, now spoke warily as if they were afraid of saying the wrong thing. They feared that they would express themselves in a way that would upset me.

On one hand, I understood how they felt, but on another level, I took it as compassion bordering on pity. At one point, I remember answering someone after they commented on how well I looked.

"Thanks. I'm grateful it isn't leprosy." I laughed when I said it, but it made me feel so disconnected from everyone else when I would hear their comments.

I knew my friends meant well, but the sense that I was no longer the same person who they had known for years chilled me. They saw me in a totally different light. I was already labeled the woman with MS (I heard someone at one of the tables say it in a whispered voice). I would later become the lady with the cane. My old fear of losing my independence and identity resurfaced. Moving back into the mainstream had not gone well for me, at least from an emotional standpoint. I realized that I had to become a tougher individual and accept the fact that I was not the same person in the eyes of the world. A bit of my foundation crumbled that morning. Had I felt a sense of false bravado until this point? Maybe I wasn't the strong-willed optimist who I believed myself to be!

I realized that for the second time in as many months that I needed to readjust my thinking. I was crawling up from some dark chasm, and once in a while I would slip, but nothing would keep me from attaining my ultimate goal! I was confident on the day that I was wheeled into the emergency room that I was going to beat this disease, and now I had to regain that positive thinking. Knowing how far I had come since then was the proof that I needed to continue my assent.

Our first home 1975

Pop and Nana holding DJ 1978

DJ, Sean, Brian 1987

Boomer 1993

Baron the Destructor 1976

Roanoke 1993-1999

Brian in the National Guard 2004

Don's mom in Roanoke

Boomer as a pup

Baron II 2005

Our home in Pittsburgh 1981-1990

Shadow

Nana Josie

Brian, Sean, DJ Christmas, 2010

# CHAPTER TWENTY-FOUR

SO MANY PEOPLE reached out to us during the winter and spring that year. We were astounded by the measure of kindness and generosity shown to our family. One of our many caring neighbors brought me a book that would become my bible. I carried that book with me as a postulant entering the convent would carry her daily order of prayers.

The book, first published in 1987, now in its third edition, is entitled *Multiple Sclerosis* by Dr. Louis Rosner and Shelley Ross. It is one of the most comprehensive volumes that I have found regarding this disease. It deals with every aspect of MS and answered all the questions that I had throughout those first months after my diagnosis and hospitalization.

The authors have explained in layman's terms what to expect from the physical, psychological, and emotional elements of MS. They have a chapter dedicated to the family of the patient and how they too are affected as a result of their loved one's disability.

The writers deal with the psychological incapacity that one encounters, which can be as debilitating as the physical consequences of the illness. In most cases, I would be pacified by the words, knowing that what I was feeling was perfectly normal for one who has been recently diagnosed.

One of my favorite and most quotable passages from their book is in the chapter entitled "Sharpening Your Emotional Tools." In it, the authors state, "The only loss to prove a real tragedy would be the loss of your sense of humor. It has been said that in MS, your sense of humor may not be the first to go, but it's the toughest to live without."

As I gained small accomplishments each week at home, my one great obstacle was the stairs. Trying to negotiate them daily proved to be exhausting. I only "climbed" them in the morning and again at bedtime.

A fellow from the human resource department in Don's company took it upon himself to contact our insurance carrier about supplying me with a chair lift. This is an apparatus that would help me to move from the first level of our home to the second floor. The device was very expensive, and the insurance company would not cover the cost of it. Bill continued to fight for our cause. He collected letters from my doctor, the therapy department, even the Multiple Sclerosis Society, which stated the need to be as important as a wheelchair in keeping a patient mobile at home as long as possible.

After four months of perseverance, Bill persuaded the company to accept our claim. We won the case and were sent a reimbursement check for the full amount. Don and I were so indebted to Bill for his tenacity in this matter.

# CHAPTER TWENTY-FIVE

AFTER SIX WEEKS at home and my first twelve sessions of outpatient therapy, I finally began to see a substantial improvement in my mobility. I was able to do more each week. I walked without the walker, only using a cane in therapy. I hadn't tried it in the "real world" yet though, not saying much about it because I wanted to surprise everyone.

One Saturday afternoon, we were all in the family room. To have everyone together in the house was a rarity. This was my best chance to show them my new skill!

I stood at the far end of the room and asked Don to come over to me. My mother was sitting at the other end reading to Brian. I announced to everyone that I was going to put my walker aside.

"My cane, sir," I said to Don in my best ringmaster's tone. I took it from him, stepped away from the walker, and moved slowly across the room toward my mother and Brian. There was a collective exhalation when I stood next to her chair. The boys cheered as I took a bow.

"How many mothers are able to see their child take her first steps twice?" My mother's rhetorical question brought laughter from the others. She and I, though, locked our eyes for a momentary impassioned look.

The boys were thrilled to see me walk on my own even if it was only a few feet and using the cane for support. In their eyes, it was quite an achievement. Don was as excited as his sons. I think that I had finally convinced my family that I was very serious when I told them over a month ago that I would walk again. After that day, I put my walker in the closet and planned to do the same with my cane soon enough.

# CHAPTER TWENTY-SIX

## April 1988

THE MONTHS OF physical therapy proved to be my salvation. As the earlier infusions of the ACTH aided in arresting the attack on my body, the PT helped me to regain the strength and coordination that I had lost.

My therapists were so supportive and diligent. I found myself working harder and pushing a bit farther because of the conviction they held onto. If these professionals believed that I was going to walk on my own again, who was I do doubt them?

I recall one session when my therapist told me that we were going to the park near the hospital. "You need to learn how to run again," she explained to me. "What if your young son runs in front of a car?"

Off we went to practice the art of running! If walking was a trial at first, running made me feel like I was starting all over again. I felt so discombobulated and clumsy, and I am sure that I looked even worse!

Stacy kept persuading me that I could do this. Each time, I would feel a bit more comfortable, but I had a long way to go before I stopped feeling like an octopus trying her land legs for the first time. Eventually, I was running well enough to convince my therapist that I could run if I needed to do so.

My last day of physical therapy was approaching. I had mastered the walker, the cane, and now being able to run again. The doctor who oversaw the department would give me my final test. He took me into a room and then shut off the lights so we were thrown into total darkness. Because I had no reference, I felt a sense of imbalance. He explained that he was performing the Romberg test. A person with MS usually has a balance problem especially with their eyes closed. This is common, he explained, and it was natural to feel an unstable effect. The assessment was in the timing, and if I could balance for a specified amount of time, I would pass, which I did! My months of therapy would soon be behind me.

Although I was walking independently for the most part while in therapy, I still relied on a cane when I was away from the hospital. One day, I asked Don to watch as I walked unaided outside where there was no temptation to grasp onto anything for support. I was literally throwing myself back into the world again. I hadn't driven on my own since that awful trip from the doctor's office, so I needed to get behind the wheel as well.

I slowly began the process of driving again as well as taking longer walks to help with strength conditioning. I even revisited DJ's classroom on the pretense of taking some papers to him. I wanted that same student who called me a cripple to see how wrong he had been to say such an unwarranted thing to my son.

The last seven months had been the most disconcerting and distressing that I would ever experience. If not for the love and never-ending support from Don, my sons' unwavering belief in their mother, and the wonderful network of family and friends who came to my aid, I would never have had the fortitude, strength, and courage it took to return to my former self.

Now that spring had arrived, my vow to walk unaided to the altar for communion at the Easter services was approaching. I was almost back to normal, but the fact that I would fulfill the promise I had made to myself all those months ago made me anxious.

I truly felt a rebirth in both body and spirit during this Easter season. I knew in my heart that I could achieve my goal. I not only walked unaided down the center aisle to receive communion, but I did it in dress shoes! I committed myself to regaining my mobility, walking without help, and for the first time since the previous autumn, I felt whole again.

At some point in my journey through hell, I discovered an inner strength that had never been challenged before. I was indeed a changed person. Outside, I still dealt with the new me as I appeared to others, and I would come to grips with that in due time.

My greater compensation though was discovering the person I came to recognize from within, and I liked who I saw. Up to this point in my life, I was handed most of what I accomplished. I never had to work very diligently for my rewards, and I rarely finished what I started. Someone had always been there to push me along. These past months proved that I could rise to the challenge. I realized that I was stronger than I ever believed myself to be. I knew that if I was ever thrown into the fire again, I would be able to utilize this newly found strength to pull myself back out. I could survive.

# CHAPTER TWENTY-SEVEN

*July, 1988*

HAD IT BEEN a year since we planned our vacation? We have lived a lifetime since our stay in the "wooden house." As a family, the past year was a rollercoaster ride of emotions. Don and I realized that while we attempted to put our lives in order again, our three sons had come away from the experience with many valuable lessons. They gained a priceless understanding of the human qualities that bind us all together. I hope it is something they will carry with them throughout their lives.

We all learned the true meaning of compromise. Our family realized how quickly one's life can be broadsided by an illness. Fortunately, in my case, it was a manageable progression, and my prognosis was within my capability. I knew what I could handle and what needed to change in order to sustain my quality of life.

Of course, the boys wanted to repeat the grand time that they had the previous year. They truly enjoyed the "bayou" and the crabs that they hauled in each day.

I reminded them of the heat on the coast and its ultimate result.

"Remember, guys, we don't want to overheat this old body. We all know what can happen." I tried to say it in an upbeat tone of voice without sounding as if I was uttering an ultimatum. I suggested that this may be the summer we explore another (and cooler) vacation site. I was so proud of their reaction to our change of venue. When they recalled what had transpired the previous vacation, they wholeheartedly agreed that this was the best idea and immediately began throwing suggestions out as to where they would like to go.

Everything from the wilds of Alaska (that was the coldest region that Brian knew) to the Rocky Mountains were suggested! Their father and I laughed hardily at the many other places that were tossed out for discussion. It was finally decided that this year, our vacation would take us to the cool climate of the north rather than the dehydrating southern beaches. Niagara Falls, it was to be!

The boys had never experienced the splendor and force of Niagara Falls, so this was not just an escape from the heat but an educational trip as well. I remember poor little Brian as he stood on the ledge directly under the falls. He was literally plastered against the rock wall as we slowly threaded ourselves in a straight line. I guess the powerful spray that soaked our yellow slickers was a pretty daunting experience for a four-year-old.

We had a wonderful time in upstate New York. From the Maid of the Mist to all the touristy things to do, my health took a back seat. We put MS right where it belonged and enjoyed all the activities on vacation.

Compassion for others was another very important lesson that my children learned. They were reminded of how important those we love are to us. There was no greater means of teaching the significance of family to our sons than through my illness. Learning to place oneself aside for the comfort of another and to be considerate of that other person's needs is a vital part of one's character.

"I hope your legs feel better." Until he left for college, Sean never said good night without saying those words to me!

Don set a wonderful example for his children with his unselfish love and care for me. The boys watched how many times their father put himself and his own needs on hold while he tended to mine. To this day, I know that I could ask anything of my husband or three sons, and they would drop their own agendas to come to my aid. Once again, I realize how blessed I am to have them in my life.

Throughout this entire process, I gained so much more than I lost. If I was ever to go through a crisis like this again, I know that the cards are in place, and I will be able to play the hand I am dealt. This offers me a great sense of peace.

I am accepting of my limitations. I've never become complacent about taking care of myself, although admittedly, I will push myself to the absolute boundary of my capabilities (much to Don's concerned chagrin). I do know all too well what the consequences are if I do not abide by the "rules" of MS, so I avoid the heat of the summer months, hot tubs, long walks, undue stress, late nights, and even negotiating the expanse of a mall for a day of shopping is something that I plan for in advance. (I take advantage of the handicap placard in my vehicle because after a trip to the mall, getting back to the car can prove to be a bit dicey.)

# CHAPTER TWENTY-EIGHT

*July 1989*

BY MID-1989, I had been relatively symptom free now for well over a year. In that time, I attempted to resume more of my ordinary activities. The boys were in more and more sports and school functions, and Don and I followed all of them. They still were very much aware of the disease and never hesitated to ask if I needed help with anything or do an errand upstairs in order to save me the trip.

Now that I had a good handle on the circumstances that I should avoid with MS, I was more secure in my decision making. I knew that excessive heat can throw me into an exacerbation. Moreover, there are other factors that should be avoided. Excessive fatigue, injuries, infections, and emotional stress are other contributors to an attack.

I opened up the discussion at dinner one evening of where to vacation this year. I could sense that everyone was a little wary of suggesting a place, so I started the dialogue.

"Since I know much more about this disease now than any of us knew before, and . . . ," I waited until I had everyone's undivided attention, "since you guys have really been troopers about helping me to stay healthy, should we try to rent the 'wooden house' this year?"

The whooping around the table answered my question. Don and I smiled as we had already discussed this in advance, and we decided that I would just have to give up some trips to the beach during the day if the temperatures climbed too high. I was willing to make concessions because I felt it was so important that we reward our sons for the tolerance they have exhibited in the last two years.

The first thing I did the following morning was to locate the information about the realtor who we had used and call to inquire on the status of that particular property. Unearthing the information and contacting the rental office was the easy part. Describing the house we had rented without an address proved to be more difficult. The address I gave the agent was not on record in the office.

After about thirty minutes of exchanging information with the woman, we were no closer to finding the house. She had a good laugh when I told her how important the "wooden house" was to my family and what a great time we had there.

"Why don't I investigate it further this afternoon and give you a call back?" Anne, the rental agent suggested to me. I agreed and told her to not hesitate to call if she needed any other information from me.

Several hours later, she called me back. The original people had sold the cottage last year, and the house was not on the list of offered properties any longer. She offered to send me a listing of what was available so we could look at them online and decide what looked good to the family.

The accommodations that we settled on could not compare with our crabbing canal, but it was close to the beach and had central air-conditioning, which was a necessity this time. The only drawback was the second story entrance, which meant a flight of stairs to enter, as this condo was close to the beach so it was built on pilasters.

We arrived in time to check in and still have an hour or so to go to the beach. The kids grabbed their towels and were changed and ready by the time Don had the remainder of the luggage unloaded. I sent him off with the boys while I stayed behind to unpack.

The weather was much more tolerable this year with temperatures in a comfortable summer range. Even with that advantage, I was very careful of the amount of times that I climbed the stairs, and if the boys wanted to stay longer on the beach with Don, I would return to the condo and relax in the air-conditioning with a good book.

It was Wednesday, midweek already, and I was feeling great. What a difference this year was now that I knew the "rules of the game." I did a fair amount of walking in the evenings. With the ocean breeze and the cool night air, I didn't think there was a risk to my health.

## CHAPTER TWENTY-NINE

FRIDAY MORNING WAS rainy, so we did the laundry and packed most of the luggage. We had a seven-hour drive the next day, so we took advantage of the down time. When the weather cleared by afternoon, we were ready to spend the last hours of our vacation on the beach.

We ate at a well-known Italian restaurant not far from our condo. The food was delicious and the servings were large enough that we took the remainder back to snack on later. A movie and leftover lasagnas rolls, what could be better than that? We all turned in early for our trip home.

About three in the morning, I got up to use the bathroom. I realized after several "tries" that I was not able to empty my bladder! In doing all my research about MS, I recalled that bladder problems were not uncommon to a person with multiple sclerosis. Most often, MS patients' problems result from urgency rather than retention though. Maybe this had nothing to do with the disease. No matter what strange episode occurred, I automatically assumed it is caused by the MS.

By the time everyone was up in the morning, I still had not been able to empty my bladder. It had been eight hours since I did, and now I was becoming concerned. I better not drink anything more; I had a seven-hour drive ahead of me!

Of course, I told Don what was happening (or wasn't), and his suggestion was to stay and seek medical attention. I knew of nowhere to go on a Saturday other than the local hospital's emergency room, and that may take hours to be seen.

I decided not to drink anything more, get on the road and plan to stop along the way. With any luck, this was a temporary situation that would resolve itself. We packed the remainder of our things, dropped the condo's key off at the realtor's, and headed home.

I tried to keep my mind on anything else but my bladder, but of course, like the proverbial corn kernel stuck in one's tooth, the tongue continually seeks it out. My mind thought of nothing else. Numerous stops at the rest areas proved futile, so we continued our journey.

I was closing in on twelve hours since my last successful trip to the bathroom. At this juncture, I was beginning to become uncomfortable to say the least. We've been on the road for a bit over four hours. I suggested that since it was almost noon, let's stop for lunch and a bathroom break (ugh). We had another three hours or so before we arrived back in Pittsburgh.

I wondered if I should call Dr. Levitt and describe to him what I was experiencing in hope that he would have an immediate solution for me. Since I have been doing so well, I only saw him twice a year now. Also, this may not even be related to MS and maybe nothing more than a Urinary Tract Infection. We continued our trip, but by the time we were within an hour of home, I was in extreme discomfort.

Don and I made the decision to call his parents from the next rest stop to make certain that they would be home when we arrived. We dropped the boys off to their grandparents and headed for the emergency room.

It was now almost sixteen hours since I discovered the problem, and several hours more since I was actually able to empty my bladder. The attending physician ordered a catheterization before he even took any other information from me. I could redefine the word "relief"! Unfortunately, my bladder difficulty was only part of my problem.

Dr. Levitt was called in after the ER doctor examined me and realized that I had lost the strength in my left leg! He told me that he thought it was best to admit me for further evaluation and to start me on the proper medicine therapy.

I remained in the emergency room, waiting for a room assignment.

"You better call your parents and let them know what is happening." Don left the room to call his parents. I could not believe that this was happening again. I thought that I could prevent a reoccurrence by being vigilant on vacation, but I was sorely mistaken! My greatest fear was that this time, my problems could be worse or even permanent!

I held my tears until Don left the room, and I needed to pull myself together before he returned. I felt so defeated. Not only my leg was affected, but my bladder was involved now also. Don walked into my room accompanied by a nurse.

"We have a room assignment for you," she told me. "I am going to gather your things together and take you upstairs."

Finally, I was moved to a room on the third floor. My roommate was an older woman who, according to the nurse, had just had surgery to remove a large portion of her stomach due to a malignant tumor.

"This is her second bout with cancer," she told me. "I had her as a patient the first time, and she is just a joy. You would never know how grave her condition is this time."

Her granddaughter was with her when the nurse wheeled me into the room. The young woman was pinning a large button on her grandmother's hospital gown that read "*Shit Happens*"! The older woman was laughing so hard about the pin that she never heard me enter the room. When she realized that we were there, she called over to my side of the room to show her pin to us.

"Isn't this a hoot?" she asked.

The nurse introduced me to the woman and her granddaughter. I couldn't help but observe her wonderful upbeat attitude. I berated myself and my negative mind-set, thinking, "You have absolutely nothing to complain about! Stop feeling sorry for yourself."

I believe that we are surrounded by those who will help us the most when we are in need. This woman was placed in my life to show me just how insignificant my current plight was compared to what she was going through. She would become my catalyst.

My schedule of hospital events replicated my last visit. However, because my prognosis was far better than in the previous attack, Dr Levitt started me on a course of oral steroids rather than the intravenous ACTH and combined it with physical therapy. The difference this time was that along with Dr. Levitt, my neurologist, I also saw the urologist on staff for my bladder retention.

I recognized that Don and the three boys were less apprehensive about this latest occurrence. Fear of the unknown was no longer a factor because they were all aware of what had transpired the first time that I was hospitalized and the eventual positive outcome. It gave them a sense of relief and encouragement this time. I wanted to believe the same, and their hopeful demeanor helped mine greatly.

Being the admitting physician, Dr. Levitt kept in constant touch with Dr. Ferber, the urologist who diagnosed my new condition as *ischuria*, which basically means lacking the ability to urinate. He concurred with Dr. Levitt's findings that my urological trouble was caused by MS.

Dr. Ferber performed a procedure that he felt would take care of my urinary problems, which it did for a short period of time. He also prescribed two different medications in hope that my urinary muscles would, in time, take over their duties naturally. One of the prescriptions was Prazosina, a drug usually used to treat high blood pressure, but in rare cases, also used in the treatment of urinary hesitancy. He combined it with another medication that he hoped would jump start the urethral sphincter. This second prescription was a dilating medication to help open the constriction in my bladder muscles, permitting them to perform normally again.

Don's parents came to the house to stay with their grandsons, and Nana Josie was awaiting her call to duty if I had a longer stay in the hospital than expected. Once again, my friends and neighbors joined forces to make certain that the boys had rides to all of their scheduled activities.

## CHAPTER THIRTY

MY HOSPITAL STAY was less than a week this time, which I took as a good sign that my recovery would also be shortened. This latest attack was nowhere near the magnitude of the previous one. Physical therapy was on an outpatient basis again. For now, I was using the walker, but my therapist assured me that within the month, I would graduate to a cane. I was even able to drive myself to outpatient therapy, given the fact that it was my left leg that was affected this time.

I began the two medications for my bladder after my release from the hospital and was to continue them until I saw Dr. Ferber for my follow-up appointment. Less than twenty-four hours after I returned home, however, I began to bleed uncontrollably. Now what?

I determined that it was a gynecological problem and called Dr. Weston, my gynecologist. When I explained what was happening, she advised me to come into her office immediately. Once again, I had to summon Don to drive me for this latest medical emergency!

By the time I was taken back into her exam room and into the dressing room, I began to hemorrhage. I called for the nurse, and when she witnessed what was happening, she beckoned the doctor. Her office was in the adjoining medical building, so I was immediately transferred to the hospital to undergo a D & C. This is common surgical procedure used to remove some of the uterine lining to establish the cause of abnormal bleeding. Dr. Weston could not determine any cause and was baffled by the unexpected intensity of the bleeding. I was discharged seven hours later and told that she wanted me to return to her office the following afternoon when all the pathology results would be available.

For the remainder of the evening at home and into the night, I continued to lose blood although not at the previous rate. I recognized that something was still wrong. I knew very little about a D & C other than this amount of bleeding was unusual after this procedure.

Before I called the doctor's service, I remembered the urologist explaining that the medication he prescribed was being used to dilate my bladder. Common sense told me what was happening! The sudden and continual bleeding was due to the medications. Instead of dilating those muscles of my bladder, the Slo-Bid was causing a reaction in my uterus! I have taken four 200mg tablets of the drug the last eighteen hours as Dr. Ferber prescribed. This medication contains theophylline, a bronchodilator, used primarily to relax and open the airways in the lungs. The combination of the two precriptions was causing a reaction. I grasped what was happening and stopped the drugs immediately! Within five hours, the bleeding stopped completely, and I never had another problem like that again.

At my follow-up appointment with Dr. Weston the next day, I explained that the bleeding had continued and how I finally realized what was happening. She would not confirm or deny my findings even though the end result was proof positive. The fact that she could not establish a reason for the sudden hemorrhaging in the first place and the need for the D&C seemed to me, more proof of a prescribing error. Dr. Weston would still not agree that I was correct.

"These things happen once in a while for no reason," she told me. "I have performed this procedure on many women without a specific cause."

She did consent to discuss it with Dr. Ferber, although the doctor again made it clear to me that she was not in accord with my conclusions. In the end, my problem was charted and filed away. I guess malpractice really is a threatening complication in the medical community.

My bladder problem was definitely MS related, and after a year of continued trials of medication to solve it, no more could be done. Those muscles will always remain paralyzed.

# CHAPTER THIRTY-ONE

*January 1990*

JUST AFTER THE holidays, Don was contacted by a firm in Marietta, Ohio, and offered an upper management position with the company. After much discussion and deliberation, we polled the family and decided to make the move. As a career opportunity, it was a good decision on Don's part. As for me, I felt that I was ready to move on with my life in an entirely different direction. I knew that I wanted to transform everything that I could about my past. It is said that within five years of a catastrophic event in one's life, a major change takes place. This was my chance for a new beginning.

I was given this opportunity to start over again in a town where no one shared any first-hand knowledge of my disability; a new environment where all I would be known to anyone is the new person in the neighborhood, not the lady with MS, not the woman with a disability. I could immerse myself in activities that had absolutely nothing to do with MS!

We found a wonderful location across the Ohio River from Don's new company. Vienna, West Virginia, is a small town with a population of approximately twelve thousand residents. Our realtor showed us numerous houses, but in the end, we decided to build our home.

Don began his new job while the rest of the family stayed in Pittsburgh to finish the school year. DJ was in his first year of middle school, Sean was in third grade, and Brian was attending kindergarten. Because the house would not be ready in time for us to move before the new school year started, our only option was to find a rental property until it was completed.

Exploring every avenue there was in search of a house to lease, Don and I were becoming more and more stressed. There was absolutely nothing available. He had contacted several realtors, but so far, there were no rental properties to be had that fit our criteria. We were not particularly choosy other than needing a short-term lease, close to the area that we would be living so the boys would be near their new schools, room for the five of us, furnished, pet-friendly . . . well, I guess we were being a bit selective!

Finally, a person who worked with Don knew of someone who knew someone else whose family would rent their home on a month-to-month basis. This sounded a bit bizarre to us, but we were getting desperate about our timing, so we agreed with certain terms. The homeowner would need a rental agreement written by our realtor protecting both parties. We would not enter into anything that was not spelled out as we hardly knew the person who first suggested this no less the third party who owned the property!

The owners of the rental house, the Grossmans (we would come to realize how aptly named), agreed to the arrangement and met with our realtor in their home. We were told that he and his wife were planning a long-term vacation and that the house would be vacant for the next several months. Don met the realtor at the property the following day and signed his part of the agreement. The next step was to schedule the moving company and secure a date to transfer our furniture into storage. The remainder of our clothes was packed as if we intended to take an extended vacation ourselves.

I decided that since we finally had a definitive moving date now, I would register the boys in school. Sean and Brian were starting school at Greenmont Elementary, and DJ was entering the seventh grade in Jackson Junior High.

Our first stop was to the elementary school. Mr. Bertram, the principal, could not have been friendlier.

"Sean, I want to welcome you," he began. "Fourth grade is a very important year, you know." He went on and on about Sean taking advantage of his time here at Greenmont. I could tell that Sean had politely tuned out his new principal. After about ten minutes, I started to wonder what point Mr. Bertram was trying to make and why he was choosing his words so carefully. Finally, he hesitantly said, "Sean, I guess what I am trying to say is that you will need to choose your friends wisely this year."

I thought "Uh oh!" What Mr. Bertram was really trying to say is that Sean could easily fall in with some less than "studious" peers. Evidentially, there were already some problems in his grade; otherwise, I was sure that this wouldn't be the most important fact to share with us about the school! I did not think this was the time to gather details, but the warning signs were there!

"If at any point, Mr. Bertram, you would feel that we should be made aware of anything with Sean, please don't ever hesitate to call his father or me." Hopefully, he realized that I understood what he was trying to convey to me.

When we finally had Sean and Brian registered, we headed for the Junior High. We stopped for lunch before finding DJ's school to enroll him. Once again, we felt very welcomed, and the first thing that his new principal did was to locate a student to take DJ on a tour of the school. Meanwhile, Mr. Smeel, the principal, planned to draw me a "map" in order to help us find our way across town. He drew his first line representing the school's parking lot. He had us turn left . . . hesitate, hesitate . . . then he started once again in a different direction. At this point, the student greeted my son and took him on his tour! After about ten minutes, Mr. Smeel had us on what he believed was the correct road, but then he wavered again. Another ten minutes elapsed, and DJ returned. He took a look at the map and realized that we had only progressed two blocks from the original starting point! I could see the flicker of a grin starting and knew exactly what my son was thinking. I knew that making eye contact with DJ was not the thing to do. We did eventually find our way out of the school's parking lot.

All kidding aside, we were very impressed with the junior high principal and the warm and inviting manner in which we were welcomed to Jackson Junior High. We thanked him and assured him that if we got lost, we would just retrace our steps back to the school.

With the boys registered in school, I felt less apprehensive about the move. Doing this took the edge off our initial experience in finding a rental house. I was sure everything would be smooth sailing from this point of in our adventure!

# *CHAPTER THIRTY-TWO*

*August 1990*

MOVING DAY HAD finally arrived, and we were packed and ready to go. We stood in the cul-de-sac and said good-bye to all our friends in the neighborhood. It was a bittersweet farewell. For the three boys, this house was the only home that any of them remembered, so they were leaving with many good memories. Although we had great times here, I was anxious to move on. I felt badly that I could not rise above this mind-set. I guess the neighborhood represented negative feelings for me even though the neighbors had been wonderful during my illness.

We packed the clothing and essentials that we would need for the next month or so, gathered Brandy, our Yorkshire terrier, and hit the road! Two hours later, we pulled into the driveway of the rental house. Don's new company was having its annual family picnic later that afternoon, so we decided that he should take the boys. In the meantime, I could unpack our things and settle in. We found the key that the realtor had left for us in the mailbox and unlocked the front door.

I cannot describe the shock when we entered the living room! It looked as if the occupants glanced at their watches and realized that they were supposed to have left hours ago! Empty glasses were on the table, a half-empty bag of chips lay open on the sofa, and a magazine was thrown on the floor next to the television!

If we weren't rendered speechless at this sight, we rounded the corner from the hallway that led into the kitchen! There were empty pizza boxes on the counter with soiled paper plates and napkins thrown in them! The kitchen sink was filled with dirty dishes; half-empty cups and glasses sat on the counter!

The place was a pigsty, and this was just the beginning of the tour! Next, we ventured down the hall past the bathroom (a wet towel hung over the door) to the bedrooms. The disgust I felt was bubbling up inside me. The beds were not made up with clean linens; as a matter of fact, the beds were not made up at all! The acrid smell of soiled sheets was palpable.

Don saw the look on my face and decided that the boys should probably walk Brandy in the yard after the long trip! What were we going to do now? All our furniture was in storage; we had a month's worth of our clothing and belongings with us and nowhere else to stay. Our first call was to the realtor, whose voice message asked us to please leave our name and number and she would return our call promptly! That was not going to happen on a Saturday afternoon. We had about as much chance of anything occurring this weekend than we had of a Molly Maid crew showing up at the door.

We had no choice but to make the best of it and try to make a livable home out of this squalor! I wanted everything to go smoothly as this was a big transition for the boys: a new town, new schools, new friends . . . and this was definitely not my definition of "smooth"!

"Look," I told Don, "why don't you and the boys go to the picnic." He started to object, but I continued, "They are looking forward to it. Go see if there is a laundry room somewhere that I can wash all the bedding and have things in some sort of order by the time you come back."

With that, he headed for the basement and I to the kitchen. I found trash bags in the cabinet and scooped all the cans, bottles, and empty pizza boxes into them. Next, I loaded the dishwasher with the dirty plates and glasses. My mood was brightening a bit.

Don announced that he found the washer and dryer downstairs with detergent and bleach on the shelf above them. "OK," I thought. "We can do this! A little extra work, and by night, we will be laughing at this debacle!"

After the rest of the family left for the picnic, I stripped the odorous, gray sheets and blankets from all of the beds. I added the towels (even those from the linen closet) and headed for the basement.

Brandy followed me downstairs and watched as I separated the piles of bedding into manageable loads. I filled the washer to its full load capacity, added the detergent, lots of bleach, and pushed the start button. The agitator started to swish the load about in the tub, and Brandy and I headed for the stairs.

I had not placed my foot on the first step when the noise from the laundry room made me dash back in! Water was pouring out of the bottom of the washer, and the agitator had stopped turning. My first thought was to grab the dog, run up the stairs and out the front door, and never look back! I knew that was not an option, so I shut off the washer and grabbed Brandy so she would not get wet as the water started to puddle around my feet.

I ran back upstairs and then stopped. Who would I possibly call? The realtor never returned our previous call, I did not have the number of the people who owned the property (I had no desire to call the Grossmans even if I could), and my cell phone was in my purse, not with Don.

This had been the day from hell. I sat on the top basement step, held Brandy, and cried! What else could go wrong, and it was only the first day of the move! We had no idea of where we were headed, literally in some respects. Our house was not finished; we were living not only in another town but also in another state from where we were moving. Most of our possessions were inaccessible at this point, and we had to continue living in this house of horrors for another four weeks!

"Stop!" I mentally screamed to myself! "There are a lot worse things than empty pizza boxes on the counter and unmade beds. We would soon be moving into a beautiful new home. The boys have all been very receptive to the shift in their lives, and if we were going to make this work, had I not learned from my illness that attitude was everything?" I thought.

My self-recrimination calmed me to a rational point; I went back downstairs to assess the damage. The water had stopped draining out when I turned off the washer. I guess that was a good thing except now, I had a flood on the floor, a washer full of soaking sheets, and three more piles of dirty laundry on the floor! The only thing I could think of doing was to squeeze as much of the water as I could out of the linens in the machine and move them to the dryer. The remaining piles of laundry would have to go to the laundromat.

By four o'clock, I was exhausted from dragging the wet blankets into the dryer then hauling the rest of the foul bedding back upstairs to the foyer and loading it into my car. The problem was that I had no idea where we were in the town and knew no one from the area to call. I decided at that point to look for some "clean" sheets and make up the beds. Surely these people had more than one set for each bed.

That finished, I looked in the phone book for area laundromats. There were several, and given the size of the town, I guessed that they would not be far from where we were living. I called only to discover that they would be closing at five o'clock for the remainder of the weekend and would not reopen until Monday morning. I've only used laundromat services in college and emergencies but aren't they usually open twenty-four hours?

Brandy and I sat in the living room and waited for Don to return. I hope that the boys were having a good time at the picnic because my first day in this new life was surely not what I expected! I had a small pizza delivered for my dinner (having taken the phone number and a coupon from one of the discarded boxes). There was nothing more soothing then a pizza with everything on it when you need a lift!

The guys returned by early evening. They had a wonderful time and were overflowing with happy stories of some unusual people they met and the great food that they consumed all afternoon. I waited until they went off to play and regaled Don with the afternoon's events. By then, I was laughing at all that had transpired. He was so appreciative of all my efforts to make semblance of the chaos. We still had full intentions of calling the realtor on Monday morning and making her aware of the shambles we encountered upon our arrival. For now, we would use the remainder of the weekend to clean the rest of the house.

Our first few weeks flew by. We eventually connected with the realtor and explained the situation. For starters, we needed to be reimbursed for the cost of the laundromat, and we needed the name of a serviceman to repair the washer. We checked on the progress of the new house each evening when Don returned from work. It was almost finished, so hopefully, we would be able to finally retrieve our furnishings and move into our new home.

Besides starting school, both DJ and Sean played football that fall. DJ was on the junior high team, and Sean was playing for the local county rec league. This was a great way to make new friends who shared the same interests.

Early each morning, Brandy and I would drive the boys across the river (dividing the two states) to their new schools. When the weather in September cooled off, we crossed the bridge in total fog. The water temperature caused the air to become so dense that we felt as if we were driving into an abyss. Visibility was not even a tenth of a mile. The first time was frightening as the only reference I had were the taillights of the cars in front of us. Unfortunately, sometimes that was not always the case. The boys, of course, thought that it was an awesome phenomenon, and after I got used to the drive, I also found it amusing.

Brian would tag along with us to watch Sean's team practice, and one evening, he found a nest in the ground with newborn rabbits.

"Can we take them home?" he asked me. In a weak moment, I agreed. We found an old box near the entrance of the park, and Brian filled it with grass. He wanted to "adopt" all four, but that was out of the question. After practice, we asked if there was a pet store, because of course, we had to bottle-feed the little animal.

The rabbit was in his box on the counter one Saturday when we left the house to go to dinner. We did not leave it on the floor as Brandy was still young and would investigate the smell of the bunny and regrettably, that is just what happened. We never thought that this cute little rabbit could actually be a wild Jackrabbit. (Of course it was, didn't we find it in a field?) The little thing hopped out of the box, down onto the floor, and just as we suspected she would do, Brandy thought it was one of her squeaky toys. Luckily, the dog was uninspired by the rabbit, and after one fatal squeeze, left it alone. We had a fitting burial in the backyard.

# CHAPTER THIRTY-THREE

*October 1990*

OUR HOME IN Vienna was finally completed! After five very long weeks in the "House of Horrors," we moved into our new home in mid-October. We loved the area and found everyone to be so welcoming. Many of the families were transferees with G.E. and DuPont, which both had plants in this part of West Virginia. We were quickly entrenched in the neighborhood, the schools, and even our new church, where donuts served in the parish hall after mass was the spiritual incentive that roused the boys out of bed on Sunday mornings!

After the episode with Brian's rabbit in the rental house, Don promised to take him to the pet store once we were settled in our new home. One Saturday, not long after we moved, off they went in search of a replacement pet! They came home two hours later carrying a large white cardboard box with the name "Pet Palace" stenciled on the side. Brian could not wait to show me what he had chosen. They set the box on the kitchen counter as I glanced over to Don. He just shrugged his shoulders and smiled.

Brian reached in and brought out a furry animal with no ears, no tail, and sharp teeth evidently because Brian yelped when the thing bit him! Great! He quickly dropped him back into the box. I peered in and saw a brown, black, and white guinea pig staring back at me.

Since the box would not suffice, back we went to the Pet Palace to purchase a cage, a bale of bedding, water and food dishes, a book on the care of guinea pigs, and any other paraphernalia needed for this animal! The boys "christened" him Gizmo after the character in the movie "The Gremlins."

Brian soon tired of the twice-weekly cage cleanings, so it fell to me to do them. He also quickly realized that his new pet was no fun at all. When he held him, Gizmo took a chunk of skin from one of his fingers, and if left out of his cage, the animal would dart off, and it took all five of us to corner him. He was also eating his weight each day in iceberg lettuce (he preferred that over other types of greens, we discovered). Guinea pigs have a life expectancy of eight years according to the book that we purchased, so we could be looking at years of caring for this critter.

Other than our furry friend, our new home was wonderful. As I hooked the hose from our central vacuum system into the wall, Don remarked, "This is a far cry from our first house, huh?" I laughed about how far we had come from the days in our first little house in Pittsburgh and all we had done just to make it livable!

I was enjoying excellent health, and even after the stress of the pizza boxes to the demise of the rabbit, I was feeling great! We had the chairlift installed, but there were times when I would actually climb the stairs without it.

Don did a lot of traveling with his new company. The first trip took place the week after we moved in, so the boys and I were given the task of putting the house in order. I must say that they were more than patient (although I saw a few furtive eye rolls) with me when I would ask them to move the same piece of furniture three times before I was satisfied with its placement. By the time Don arrived home from his trip a week later, we had most of the boxes emptied, pictures hung, and the rooms in order.

There were a few anomalies in the new area, which we came to accept. No school bus service (unless the student lived in the far reaches of the county) meant daily carpooling. This actually worked out well for the carpool mothers who often made plans for lunch while sitting in the drop-off line. Believe it or not, we actually had hand-printed signs to hold up in our car windows with the name of the restaurant *du jour*!

Ceaseless gray skies and the acrid smell of sulfur, which permeated the air, were constant reminders of the chemical companies surrounding Vienna. We referred to the area as "carcinogenic valley." I actually held my breath when I stepped onto the porch to retrieve the newspaper as the smell of "rotten eggs" was at its worst in the morning. We literally never saw a blue sky for the duration of our time there.

I paint a rather dismal picture of the area, but the wonderful people who we have come to know and form lifelong friendships with were well worth the absence of blue skies.

# CHAPTER THIRTY-FOUR

*January 1991*

"OK, CAN YOU hear me, DJ?" Don was in Jakarta, Indonesia, over ten thousand miles from West Virginia. He was attempting to instruct DJ (at the cost of twelve dollars a minute), on the use of the snow blower! While he was away, we had a major snow storm that brought a standstill to most of the region.

Finally, after a long weekend, the roads were plowed, and the schools reopened again. The storm did not bode too well for me, however. In our neighborhood, the mail was delivered to "cluster" mailboxes. These were located down the hill from our address, and I usually would stop on my way to or from home to retrieve the day's mail. Because of the recent storm, instead of taking my car, I decided to walk to the mailbox. I slipped most of the way down, and coming back up the hill, I actually fell several times. Within a week of the mail incident, I was out of remission and walking with my cane once again.

The neurologist who treated this latest exacerbation had me come into his office twice a week for an injection of the ACTH.

The nurse administered the shot, so I never actually saw the doctor after the initial visit. This was my third flair up since the two major events in Pittsburgh. With each, I noticed not only a change in the severity but also a variance in my treatment. Whatever the difference in approach, after four weeks, I was already regaining the strength that I had lost in my leg. I knew the therapy by rote, so unless there was little improvement, I declined physical therapy. Within the first month, I saw significant improvement, and I was totally back in remission in six weeks or so. This came as a great relief to me. Being in a totally new area, knowing only a few people, and with all the traveling Don would be doing with his new position, I needed all my faculties!

# CHAPTER THIRTY-FIVE

## *Spring 1991*

MY MOTHER CAME to visit for Easter with plans to stay for her birthday in May. Nana Josie usually spent Easter with us, and I recall one particular holiday when the boys were very young. Two dozen eggs between the three of them and they were still squabbling over whose egg remained too long in a certain color or someone having an extra egg that didn't belong to them. "Someone's taking my eggs" became a household expression after DJ blurted that out in an accent that would have rivaled Don Corleone in *The Godfather*! Until this day, we hear that phrase whenever someone "borrows" anything without permission!

Nana Josie celebrated her eightieth birthday, and true to form, her statement after blowing out the candles was "Well, I am eighty now, my life is over!" We laughed but later on, we realized that maybe she had some psychic sense after all.

The weather was ready for spring flowers, and Mom was sitting on the front porch while I planted the spring flora. Our neighbors at the end of the cul-de-sac were both doctors, and when Laura stopped by to say hello, she immediately noticed that my mother's breathing was labored and her ankles were swollen.

"How long have you been breathing like this?" she asked Josie. She told Laura that she had some discomfort at night when she would lie down.

I told Laura that I noticed recently that my mother was having some problems and would lose her breath without much exertion. Her response whenever I would ask her to see a doctor here was always the same. "I'll just wait until I get home. I need to see my own doctor in New Jersey," she would tell me.

"I want you to take your mother to the emergency room right now, and I will meet you there." I was stunned by the expedient way that Laura reacted to my mother's condition.

She proceeded to explain that my mother's symptoms may indicate fluid building in her lungs. When I told her that the respiratory problems had started a few weeks before, Laura felt more certain of her preliminary speculation. I made arrangements for the boys when they returned from school and called Don at work. Fortunately, he was in town this month.

Mom was examined in the emergency room and admitted to the hospital that evening. She was not happy with the pace to which this all happened and kept telling the doctors that she was just visiting and would take care of the problem at home. When we were alone, she would say to me, "Just have them release me. I don't want to die in West Virginia. I belong in New Jersey!" She would laugh when she said it, but I knew she was masking her fear.

After a week in the hospital, my mother was diagnosed with congestive heart failure (CHF). Finally, she was released to a rehabilitation center fairly close to the house, so I was able to drop the boys off at school and then head there each day.

The doctor at the rehab center came in one afternoon while I was visiting and performed the standard battery of psychological tests. I chuckled because at one point, he stopped to remind my mother that he was the one who was asking the questions!

Mom was improving somewhat with medication, but she still insisted that she would be better off with her own doctor in New Jersey. That option looked less likely as time went on.

Her roommate in the rehab center was a woman in her early forties who had MS! She was in a wheelchair, and although she lived on her own, this latest exacerbation was severe enough that she was not able to return home without having intense therapy.

Linda had been in a chair for nearly five years. Her upper-body strength was good until this last flare-up, but now that was compromised as well. Picking up items at the store or doing things in the room for her gave me a sense of deference not just for Linda but also for the disease. It was clear that I had beaten the odds, for now anyway, and the feeling of knowing that I was able to give something back was gratifying to me.

I kept in touch with Linda for several years after I met her. She never did rebound from the last episode, however. Linda died from breast cancer in 1998.

# CHAPTER THIRTY-SIX

*August 1991*

MY MOTHER WAS being discharged from the rehab center and had to be released by eleven o'clock in the morning. Don's mother and father were coming to visit us for the first time since we moved to West Virginia, so I wanted everything to look its best. They were expected to arrive in the early afternoon.

I was hanging fresh towels in the powder room when I spied a large black ant crawling up the wall. A carpenter ant! Of course I knew exactly what it was this time having made acquaintance with them so many years before! Maybe it is only one since this room was located right next to the garage. I picked it up with a tissue and disposed of it. I actually hesitated before I got the Raid from the garage though, remembering the last time I sprayed for carpenter ants! Some memories never die!

I knew I was being ridiculous! Locating a full can of the insecticide, I proceeded to spray around the vanity, the commode, and the baseboard. Déjà vu! Ants ran up the wall behind the vanity, onto the floor around the doorway, and into the hall! I sprayed the remainder of the pesticide to stem the blitz of bugs then grabbed the phonebook and found the number of the closest exterminator.

Glancing at the clock, I realized I had only a little over an hour before I was due at the rehabilitation center to pick up my mother, and in another couple of hours, my in-laws would be arriving. I had a floor blackened with dead carpenter ants.

"Hello, is this Orkin?" I shrieked into the phone.

"Yes ma'am, how can I help you?"

As coherently as possible, I explained the situation and asked if there was anyone in the vicinity of my home who could come out right away. I know I must have sounded like a crazy lady because the woman immediately put me on hold, and less than a moment later, she was back on the line.

"I have someone who is in the Vienna area," she told me. "He is finishing with his present call and can be there in the next thirty minutes." I thanked her profusely, hung up, and headed to the powder room to clean up the dead insects.

The "bug man" was ringing the bell in less than twenty minutes. He sprayed inside and out and assured me that after a cursory inspection of the exterior walls, he found no sign of an infestation. I didn't feel much better, but at this point, I would have believed anything that I was told.

Eighty-five dollars later, I was speeding down the highway to pick up my mother. We arrived back home with just enough time to light some scented candles and spray the entire first floor with something strong enough to eradicate the odor of bug spray before my in-laws pulled in.

All's well that ends well and the remainder of my in-law's visit proved to go forth without incident. It was wonderful to see Don's parents. They loved our new home, and the subject of carpenter ants and exterminators never found its way into the conversation that weekend.

# CHAPTER THIRTY-SEVEN

## *June 1992*

IT HAD BEEN close to a year since my mother was diagnosed with CHF. She remained with us, and despite promises that she would return home to New Jersey, the possibility grew dimmer as her Congestive Heart Failure worsened. She was up most nights with her breathing difficulties, and one of the boys would come to our room if she needed me. This became more and more frequent, until finally, Don and I had to make a decision.

"Your mother needs more care than you are able to give her," he said to me one evening. "I can see the toll it's taking, and you cannot jeopardize your own health." My mother was just as unhappy knowing what the stress was doing to my condition. In the months that I took care of her, I needed two different courses of medication to stabilize my MS. I knew Don was right. I was exhausted, and the situation was not going to get any better with time. The boys were not receiving the attention they needed either.

We sat down with my mother and discussed the alternatives. She needed to consider either assisted living if she wanted to return to New Jersey or moving in with my brother and his family in Arizona. If my mother returned to her home, she would have no one there at night if she needed someone. I explained that she was not in a position to live alone anymore, but she insisted that she would have help if she would need it.

"I have people to call in an emergency, a call button in the apartment, and I am more familiar with the care there," she told us. I knew that all she wanted was to return to the familiarity of her own surroundings.

At the end of August, I took my mother home. In less than a month, I would fly back to New Jersey to make arrangements for her to move to my brother's home in Tucson. The short period of time in which she tried to remain independent proved to be disastrous. She panicked when she couldn't breathe and called the paramedics on more than one occasion.

Neil and I made arrangements for Mom to "visit" with my brother until she was able to adjust her medications to help stabilize her condition. She did not want to go across the country to live, but unfortunately at this point, my health dictated how much I could do. It broke my heart to see what this was doing to my mother. She would be leaving everyone and everything that was familiar to her and move over a thousand miles away.

My brother flew in on Labor Day weekend. We packed enough of Mom's things for an extended stay for now. This was not an easy decision, but there were no other options. I saw the defeat in my mother's face when she locked her apartment door for what would be the last time. She knew she was not coming back again. There was nothing I could say. We parted in tears at the airport terminal.

# *CHAPTER THIRTY-EIGHT*

*December 1992*

THE HOLIDAYS HAD become a bittersweet time for me since that first season after my diagnosis. This year was not only a melancholy time, but with my mother so far away, it made it even more so. I spoke with her several times a week, and she always sounded so distressed. I knew that my brother and his family were doing everything they could to make her feel comfortable and at home, but it just was not where she wanted to be. The Saturday before Christmas, we were entertaining some friends when I received a call from my brother.

"Bon, I just left the hospital," he said. "The doctor stopped Mom's medication for an out-patient procedure a few days ago, and a blood clot formed in her leg."

"How serious is it?" I asked.

"It isn't good, Bon." He went on to explain that they were trying to dissolve the clot that was stopping the circulation to her left leg. "She is also on a respirator for her labored breathing," he said.

By week's end, my mother's condition worsened to the point that there was little left to do. Her leg was becoming gangrenous from the lack of blood to the tissue. The doctors were considering the possibility of amputation! Attempts to wean her off of the respirator failed, so we had to make a decision.

I booked the first flight that was available to Tucson. DJ and Sean traveled with me in the event that I would need them especially to navigate the expanse of the airport. As it turned out, they had to run ahead to the departure gate while I rode on a tram. My brother met us at the baggage claim when we arrived.

I wanted to go straight to the hospital, but Neil thought it was better for the boys to go back to the house with their cousins. My two nieces were both younger than DJ and Sean and were looking forward to their cousins' visit.

"The real reason I'd rather drop the boys off first is that I don't think that you want her grandsons to see Nana the way she looks." He told me that he hadn't taken his girls to see her since she was admitted to the hospital.

I understood his reasoning the minute we walked into the anteroom, a small partitioned area with a window to view the patient. I peered at my mother through the glass and knew what my brother meant. She lay under the sheet with her eyes closed and a breathing tube taped to the left side of her face. Her small frail body looked surreal to me. I turned toward my brother.

"I didn't know how to prepare you for this," he said. My brother held me while I recovered from the shock of seeing our mother like this.

I entered her room and stood by the bed. Mom focused on me, and I will never forget the beseeched look that I saw in her eyes. Her mind was still very much aware, but she couldn't escape from her shattered body. I felt totally helpless. This was the person who was always so strong and confident, and now she was slowly shutting down. I took her hand in mine. Her parchment skin felt cold to my touch; her lips were dried from the ventilator. I found a swab to moisten them. I was struggling to keep my voice steady so she would not sense my utter heartache, but we were too close to one another to hide even our slightest emotions. My mother understood. I was there because she was dying. I had come to say good-bye.

# CHAPTER THIRTY-NINE

*January 28, 1993*

I WAS IN the hallway, winding the grandfather clock, when the phone rang. Eleven-eighteen. Ten years before, my mother and I sat on the hall stairway watching as the delivery men set up the new clock. We laughed at the time about who would be named in the will to inherit our prized clock. Now my brother was calling to tell me that the doctor removed the ventilator tube. I hung up the phone and sat on the hall steps again, but this time, it was with sorrow. I lost the one person who knew me better than anyone else. My mother was gone.

We brought her back to her beloved New Jersey and laid her to rest beside her sisters and brother. The January winds blew across the grave markers. The chill was matched by the loss that I felt. A chapter in my life closed that morning.

# *CHAPTER FORTY*

## March 1993

AFTER THREE YEARS in West Virginia, we were on the move again! Don's company decided that they would be more successful by closing down the facility in Ohio and moving to Roanoke, Virginia. Although we hated to once again disrupt the boys' education and start them in a new school, the location was great. The Roanoke Valley was a beautiful area.

Our newest residence sat on the corner lot of a cul-de-sac. From the exterior, it was a stately brick home that we were told was the premiere model in the original plan of homes. Time would tell that this lovely home was all "phoo-phoo" and no substance. It was shades of our very first house years before, only larger and more demanding of costly repairs.

The rear stairway from the kitchen had an oversized Palladian window that looked out to an incredible view of the Blue Ridge Mountains. One Friday afternoon, not long after we moved in, Don passed by the window on his way upstairs and noticed an area where the paint had started to peel on the sill. He decided to investigate and flaked off some of the loose paint to feel the wood. It was damp underneath the chipped area. He used a scraper to probe the bubbled paint. The tool went all the way through the sill and when the sodden wood was removed, all that remained was a gaping hole in the wall and the exposed edge of the pane of glass. The resulting damage cost an entire weekend's work, but by Sunday afternoon, after numerous trips to the hardware store and some colorful language, we had a new window sill ready for painting.

This was the precursor for the many repairs to come. With putty, paint, and luck, we were able to fix most of the damage that we continued to encounter. All the exterior window sills were crumbling due to the inferior wood that was used to construct the house originally. The sunroom, which was all wood, was slowly disintegrating. Don spent weekends replacing the door frame and much of the siding.

I remember the afternoon that DJ came home from school and climbed the stairway to his room. When he stepped into the upstairs hallway, his foot went right through the floorboard. We heard the crack all the way downstairs. The only thing that stopped his foot from going through to the ceiling below was the carpeting! The house was literally decaying under our feet! For the six years that we lived in that house, we painted, sealed, nailed, and replaced most of it. We could have written the sequel to "The Money Pit."

Some of the damage, I must admit, was our own doing. Three boys, an out-of-control dog, and my husband, the modern day answer to John Wayne, took some of the blame. Don was working in the den one evening when something flew by him. Out of the corner of his eye, he saw a huge black "bug" rocketing at full speed past his head and into the blinds behind his chair. He turned toward the window just in time to see what was crashing around the room.

"There's a bat flying around in here," he hollered up the stairs. The boys came running down in time to see the nocturnal creature crash into the lamp shade on the desk! "Get the BB gun, Brian!" Don yelled.

"A BB gun!" I gasped. What was Don thinking? Before I could say anything to stop the Wild West show from unfolding, Brian appeared in the doorway armed and loaded!

The next thing I heard was Brian telling his father that the bat was perched on the window blinds again and that his father would have a perfect shot. Oh boy! This could not be good for the bat or the blinds!

He passed the gun to his father who took aim. The shot hit the bat, which frightened him, and off he flew landing onto the lamp shade again, dripping rabid blood along the way!

I grabbed Brandy and took her out of the line of fire then found a trash bag, towel, and a broom . . . the rational way to trap a bat. I was too late though. The small mammal was no longer a threat. We scooped it up in the bag and took it outside.

When the commotion was over, Don realized that a gun may have not been the best "weapon" of choice to capture a small, blind, defenseless bat! Beside the lampshade that was ruined, there were numerous BB-sized holes in the windows and blinds. I am not sure how I would explain this to the insurance adjuster when he came to the house to assess the damage.

After the check was written for the deductible and the windows and blinds replaced, the bat story became another chapter of our family's saga. Brian learned the importance of closing the flue in the fireplace, and his father realized that a broom and towel can be a very effective way to capture a bat.

# CHAPTER FORTY-ONE

*Dogs, Dogs, Dogs . . .*

THE BOYS HAD pestered us for a "real dog" since we left Vienna. Brandy was almost five and most often was either in my arms or sleeping. She weighed only four pounds and even as a young dog, she had always been a prim and proper puppy who grew up to be a dog with an attitude when it came to anyone in the family but me. I promised that I would take them to the animal shelter just to *look* at the puppies. Sean fell in love with a small soulful-eyed puppy (They all look that way through the "bars," don't they?) He harassed us until his father finally took him back to the pound to adopt the dog.

He wanted to name his new dog Zeus, but when Don watched the puppy's antics, he laughed and said, "I don't know, Sean, he looks more like a "Boomer" to me!" So it was, the new puppy was named Boomer, and if that is the canine moniker given to an out-of-control, unmanageable, totally incorrigible dog, it fit this puppy perfectly! Boomer put "Baron the Destructor" to shame when it came to damage.

The shelter told us the unfortunate history of the puppy. Evidently, he was born and lived on the streets until someone was kind enough to take him to the shelter. This fact helped us to understand some of Boomer's strange behavior. He ate and digested anything! Carpeting, Christmas wreathes, wood, paper... nothing was safe from this Billy goat of a canine! He once devoured an entire platter of raw hamburgers waiting to be grilled for dinner. The only thing that Boomer found distasteful was sardines (we thought we would test his epicurean side)!

It was midsummer and the three boys and I planned a trip back to visit our friends in West Virginia, leaving Don with Boomer to do some male bonding for the weekend. On Sunday morning, Don went out the door in his robe to retrieve the paper when the dog charged up to the door and accidently slammed it shut. The keys were inside with Boomer, and Don was outside on the front lawn in his robe with the Sunday paper! The only neighbor who was home that morning was the one we hadn't met yet, so poor Don had to introduce himself (in his robe) to ask for the use of their phone to call a locksmith. The embarrassing and costly trip to the mailbox did not ingratiate Boomer to Don. There was little bonding that occurred that weekend.

One afternoon, Boomer ran after a car and actually had his paw partially run over by the car's rear tire. The driver felt much worse than Boomer, who went loping off to find something else to distroy while we consoled the distraught driver!

Brandy never accepted Boomer. He certainly demanded everyone's attention, and until his arrival, she had been the canine queen. (No one paid attention to Gizmo except when the refrigerator door opened, and he would squeal for his lettuce.)

One Saturday evening not long after Boomer's arrival, we were sitting on the rear patio when suddenly Brandy ran across the yard to the driveway behind us. The owner was backing his car out of his garage, and Brandy, not sensing that the car was actually backing toward her, ran underneath the rear bumper! It all happened so quickly that by the time we got to her, she had already lost consciousness. We rushed her to the emergency clinic, where she lasted through the night. The vet told us that he could put a pacemaker in our Yorkie in the hope that the swelling in her brain had not caused permanent damage. We had to make the awful decision to have our dog euthanized. Brandy was put to sleep on Brian's tenth birthday, five years to the day that we brought her home from the breeder.

Don knew how close I was to Brandy and how much I missed her. She went everywhere with me, and weighing only four pounds, she was always in my arms around the house. I even was able to conceal her if I ran into a store for something! Unbeknown to me, he called the breeder where we had purchased Brandy, but she had no pups on-site or due this season.

One weekend, we were at the mall, and as always, stopped into the pet store to see the variety of puppies on-hand. They had two little Yorkshire terriers, one male and one female. They were adorable, but I was not ready to replace Brandy. We talked to the woman who told us that her puppies came from Oklahoma and were fully certified with papers and lineage. I told Don that I had to think about it, and if we were supposed to adopt one of these pups, the dog would be there when we made our decision.

Several weeks passed, and I decided to call the woman in the pet shop.

"Is the female Yorkie still available?" I asked. The shop owner told me that the male was adopted already, but that the female was still there. We brought our new little Yorkshire terrier home that weekend. Because Brandy had been my shadow, the boys thought that it was apropos to name the new puppy "Bonnie's Shadow."

The woman failed to mention that her Oklahoma "breeder" was a puppy mill! When the vet checked Shadow, he asked us what breeder she came from. When we told him that she was from a pet store, he said "Oft times these dogs are from out of state, and the local regulations do not apply." He found that Shadow had inherent problems with her knees. "It's unlikely that she will ever be able to jump like a normal Yorkie," he told us.

We could accept that, but a week later, the puppy started to have wrenching coughing spells, making her whole little body shudder. I called the woman at the pet store.

"Sounds like kennel cough," she said in a matter-of-fact tone of voice.

"What can I do for her? She is so distressed when she coughs so hard."

"Not much . . . she should outgrow it." Three weeks later, when the coughing continued, I called her again. She became irritated with me and said, "Bring her back, and I will have her euthanized!" I could not believe what I was hearing. This woman's attitude was reprehensible. The vet was able to give Shadow an expectorant for the worse episodes, but the intensity had permanently damaged her trachea. We certainly learned our lesson about checking supposed "papers" for a puppy.

Shadow truly became a shadow and bonded with no one. When she needed something, only then would she make herself visible! We often laughed and said we should have named her "Anita = I need a . . ." She was diagnosed with cancer several years before she died but finally succumbed to a stroke when she was almost seventeen years old.

Meanwhile, Boomer continued his reign of terror, destroying and digesting everything he could eat when out of our sight! We finally decided that obedience school would be in Boomer's best interest, so he was enrolled in an eight-week course. Because baseball season was underway, I was elected to take the dog to class each week.

The group met outside in the parking lot of a small shopping center. The first session was an hour of "getting to know your dog." This would give the trainer an idea of what each dog needed to learn. We paraded the animals around in a circle, with the trainer yelling commands to the owners.

Boomer seemed to take offense to this because he did the complete opposite of whatever he was instructed to do. When I told Boomer to sit, he would lie down on the ground and throw his legs in the air! When I gave the command "down," Boomer broke loose and traumatized the other dogs in the group. The "heel" command prompted Boomer to empty his bladder, leaving a puddle in the circle.

By the second week, Boomer was no better. Spring weather was unpredictable, and the temperature was still hovering at ninety degrees at six-thirty that evening, so we were all moving a bit slower around the infamous circle. While the other animals were catching onto the commands, my dog was behaving like the class clown! Finally, after disrupting the class once too often, the trainer asked his assistant to take Boomer from me. All the other dogs and their owners retreated to the nearest shade while Boomer was made an example of on the hot pavement.

This went on for the next twenty minutes until the class ended. Everyone headed for air-conditioned cars with their panting dogs. Poor Boomer was totally bedraggled and confused, with his tongue hanging to the side of his mouth. I helped him into the car and blasted the air-conditioning vents directly on him. I had to get him back to the house and rehydrated quickly!

I pulled into the garage and opened the rear door, but Boomer would not move to climb out of the back seat! Finally, I called DJ, and together, we maneuvered the dog out of the car and into the kitchen. We gave him a cool bowl of water, but the poor dog could not even stand up at this point. DJ picked him up and laid him in his crate while we tried to figure out what was going on with him. After fifteen minutes of coaxing Boomer to take some water, we knew something was drastically wrong.

"You stay here with him and try to get him to drink some water," I told DJ, "I have to pick up Sean from baseball practice."

Don was out of town on business, so I was mentally listing my options as I drove to the ball field. What vet would be open at eight in the evening? I had never used the emergency service for our current vet, but we would have to call if there was no change.

Sean was surprised when I drove into the field without Boomer in the car.

"Uh oh." He laughed when he saw me alone in the car. "What did Boomer do now?" Sean thought his dog was being punished for another infraction and didn't get a ride to the ball field.

"Sean, I think there is something wrong with Boomer," I began. "I'm afraid that we are going to have to find a vet that will see him tonight." I told him about the heat and how Boomer had been made an example by the trainer. "DJ and I have tried to get him to drink something, but he is not responding at all."

I pulled into the driveway, and Sean jumped out of the car before I even stopped. When I parked and entered the kitchen, the two boys were on the floor trying to get the dog to respond to them. There was absolutely no movement in the cage. I immediately grabbed the phone book and called the veterinary office. The answering service told me that he used an after-hours clinic on the other side of town and gave me the phone number and directions. I called and made arrangements to have Boomer seen that evening.

We placed the dog's crate in the car and followed the directions. As soon as the vet looked at Boomer's condition, he knew that he was suffering from heat prostration.

"He is definitely not responding," the vet explained, "but there is a chance that if I can get some fluids into him quickly enough, we can prevent his organs from shutting down." He took him in the back, and we waited for what seem like an infinitesimal amount of time.

When he finally reappeared, he looked grim and said "I've started an IV. All we can do is pump fluids into him and hope that his kidneys have not sustained too much damage." Then he asked how this happened. I explained to him what had transpired earlier in the evening.

The vet was appalled at the handler's treatment of Boomer. He offered to write a letter accusing the business of mistreating the animals in their care. "Depending on what happens over night," the doctor told us, "I think that you should take this further." I knew what he was referring to, but I hoped that it would not come to that, and tomorrow, Boomer would be his crazy old self again.

I was there when the veterinarian's office opened at nine o'clock the next morning. The receptionist led me into the doctor's office. Another interminable wait, until finally, the vet appeared. I knew that the news about Boomer was bad as the doctor came over and sat in the chair next to me instead of behind his desk.

"I just checked on Boomer again. He has deteriorated since my last check an hour ago. His pupils are dilated, and I am afraid there is nothing more I can do at this point. I'm sorry."

I was speechless. The poor animal did not deserve this! It seemed that Boomer was doomed from birth, but I was comforted to know that at least he had over a year of happiness with us. He was Sean's constant buddy, never straying far from his "rescuer's" side. Every afternoon, he would run to greet the boys when he heard the school bus coming up the hill. He traveled in the car no matter where we were heading and would lay in the rear window ledge to watch the people in the cars behind us. With all that he destroyed in the time he was with us, he still was a loveable dog who did not deserve to die at the hands of a negligent trainer!

The fragmented memories of Boomer popped into my mind as I waited for the staff to process the paperwork for me to sign. The doctor asked if I wanted to see Boomer before he took him away, but I declined. He must have seen my expression and reached over for a box of tissues as he patted my hand.

The remainder of the weekend was a depressing time. Sean worked through his grief, and by Sunday afternoon, he was more angry than sad and was ready to pursue a lawsuit against the owner and his obedience school.

He went with me to the following week's class to explain what had happened to Boomer. Evidently, the owner of the school had already heard about Boomer's fate and subsequently asked every one of the other dog owners in the class to sign a statement saying that Boomer climbed into the car of his own accord. Whatever happened to him was not a result of his mishandling of the dog. All but one person signed his account of what had occurred.

We never brought a lawsuit against the handler, but I believe we could have won the case. In the end, legal proceedings would not have brought Boomer back; we healed and moved on, left with crazy, wonderful memories of our hobo dog.

# CHAPTER FORTY-TWO

WE CONTINUED TO make never-ending repairs to the house. The boys settled into their school activities and sports. It had been months now since we lost Boomer, but we still laughed about some of his antics and the joy that he brought to our family. Nevertheless, being a one-dog/one guinea pig family again had it perks. The boys were all busy with school activities, so no one had time to "bond" with a new pet.

I picked up Brian from his friend's house one afternoon, and as I drove up to the house, I saw him jumping around in the driveway, very animated about something.

"Uh oh," I thought. I soon found out why when the boys ran to my car window. The neighbor's dog had a litter of puppies that were now six weeks old, and Brian and his friend had played with them all afternoon!

"Mom, just come over and look at them," Brian begged! I agreed to walk across the lawn and ***just look*** at the crate of puppies in the garage.

"I don't think we are ready for another dog right now, Brian," I told him.

"I know. I just want you to see them." I've seen that angelic, wide-eyed look before. In the corner of the garage, under a pile of blankets were three puppies, each one completely different in appearance. One looked like a miniature Pomeranian, another the same size as the first but white with brown markings, and the third puppy was a carbon copy but with black markings in the same area.

Just then a woman came out of the side door. "Hi," she held out her hand. "I'm Carol. You must be Brian's mother."

"Oh boy, she already knows my son by name and acts as if she was expecting me!" I introduced myself and shook her outstretched hand.

"I notice that you have seen three of the puppies already. They are actually my granddaughter's who lives in Virginia Beach," she explained without hesitating. "She is away on vacation, so I am dog sitting for the week."

This was much more information than I needed to know just to look at her puppies. I smelled a rat, as they say.

Brian came running over with a fourth puppy in his arms. This dog looked entirely different than the other three in the crate. By now, I was questioning the paternity of these pups.

Carol went on to enlighten me about the litter. They were all adopted, she said, and as soon as they were weaned, she would be releasing them to the new owners.

"That's fine," I told her. "We are not looking for a new pet right now. Anyhow, these dogs are going to be pretty big judging by their size at six weeks! The only one I would even consider is the small one that Brian is holding, but as I say, we are really not interested right now."

Carol continued her sales pitch as if I had not spoken. "He is the runt of the litter," she said. Her female German shepherd is the mother of the pups. "This one's father was a Rottweiler, and that is why the vet cropped his tail." I nodded, trying to show as little interest as possible without being rude. "If you leave your number, as I said, they are all spoken for, but you never know until the people actually pick them up . . ."

Brian rattled off our phone number, and before I could reiterate the fact that we were not in the market for a dog right now, Carol pulled a scrap of paper from her pocket and jotted it down.

Every few days for the next weeks, Brian would mention the dog.

"I guess the people took the dog, Mom," he would tell me in a crestfallen voice. "It's been almost two weeks."

"We talked about this, Brian," I said to him. "You heard what the lady told us. The puppies were all adopted, and she did not expect the people to back out." I attempted to disguise the relief that crept into my voice. For the first time in years, I had my health back. The care of a new puppy was not something that I wanted to take on right now. I was working part time; the boys were in school. Who was going to take care of the dog during the day and take the time to train him?

Another week and a half went by. I was sure that the pups, over nine weeks old now, have gone to their new owners.

School began in less than two weeks, and Sean, Brian, and I were shopping for clothes and school supplies one Saturday afternoon.

When we returned to the house, DJ walked into the kitchen and said, "Mom, Carol somebody just called and said we can pick up the dog?"

Brian was ecstatic, but I quickly stifled his excitement. "Brian, we haven't even talked about taking this dog. Dad knows nothing about it, and by the way, when was the last time you thought to clean Gizmo's cage?" I asked.

"I will be totally responsible for this dog, Mom. Please, can we go ask Dad?" Don was at the high school building new equipment lockers for the football team. After another thirty minutes of listening to Brian plead and cajole, I relented and drove him over to the school to ask his father. I knew Don would be in my corner on this one.

"I don't know, Brian. You haven't shown much care with Gizmo," Don said as if reading a script we'd prepared earlier. I saw the look of disappointment in Brian's face, but he had anticipated his father's reaction and quickly came up with a response.

"You cannot compare that guinea pig with a puppy, Dad. Look at the fun we all had with Boomer." The next thing I heard was Don making a deal with Brian that he could have this dog, but he would take complete responsibility for the dog's care when he was home. "Mom will be there during the day while you are in school."

I thought, "Well, this was not going well, and was "Mom" consulted about this deal?" Somehow our eleven-year-old was outmaneuvering his father and winning the argument. Don looked at me and shrugged as if to say, "What could I say?" I thought "no" would have been an appropriate response.

Does anyone but me remember the trauma to Brandy or the sadness we felt after Boomer died? Obviously, time heals all wounds, and we were back to a two-dog, one-guinea-pig family again.

Carol was waiting for us when we drove up to her house. The little pup was squirming in her arms and eager to take off through the yard toward our car. Brian jumped out with Sean behind him. She had a small collar on the puppy, and I had to admit that he was cute. She handed us the small leash, and the boys snapped it on the puppy's collar. They put him down on the driveway where he immediately emptied his bladder on the side of my shoe. Welcome to the family, little guy. Carol handed me a bag of dog treats and a can of food and thanked me for taking the last of her granddaughter's litter.

"The family who was originally taking the puppy reneged," she said as the boys ran their new dog around the driveway. "I was fortunate to still have your number." I just smiled.

Brian named his new puppy Rocky, and thankfully, Shadow accepted his arrival much better than Brandy welcomed Boomer! Brian and Rocky were inseparable. He kept his promise to Don and took full responsibility for his new dog (except when he was gone all day for school, of course!).

Rocky was an intelligent dog and quickly learned the acceptable behavior in the house. Unfortunately though, the mix of Rottweiler and German Shepherd made him extremely territorial, which posed a problem for anyone who did not belong to our family! He bit several people in the neighborhood, not badly enough to bring a lawsuit against us, but most of our neighbors quickly learned not to approach him if we weren't nearby. When he was outside with us, Rocky sat at the edge of the driveway like a stone figure; the sentinel who forced most people to walk on the other side of the street.

I was happy to come home from work one evening and announce that I had found a new home for Gizmo. He was an old man of seven now, still not trained to do much more than screech each morning for his breakfast of lettuce and consequently need his bedding cleaned at least three times a week depending on his consumption. A family with three young children and no yard for a dog thought it was the perfect solution to their desire to adopt an animal. He learned to be handled without biting and had the run of their house. Our guinea pig lived for another year with his new family. Gizmo finally died in his eighth year, fairly close to the timeline given in our *Enjoying Your New Guinea Pig* book.

# CHAPTER FORTY-THREE

AFTER ALL THAT had transpired with the animals and the house, I still remained in remission. Nevertheless, I needed to establish myself with a neurologist in the event that I would need medical care sometime in the future. Dr. Hilbrandt was recommended to me by a neighbor. He had treated her husband for nerve damage after an auto accident. She had the utmost regard for the neurologist.

When I met Dr. Hilbrandt, I understood what my neighbor meant about his professional manner, his knowledge of neurology, and his caring attitude toward his patients. For the first time since I left Dr. Levitt's practice, I felt a sense of confidence in my doctor.

On July 23, 1993, a promising new drug was approved by the FDA. I recalled Dr. Rosen stating in his book that there would be a breakthrough in the treatment of MS within the next several years. This was it! The name of the new medication was Betaseron, and the neurological community was eager to have their patients registered to try this new medical advance.

Betaseron was hailed as the first viable solution in combating the effects of multiple sclerosis. Although not a cure for MS, the new drug was designed to decrease the number of exacerbations, therefore stemming the progression of the disease. It is prescribed for those patients who are relapsing-remitting and still ambulatory. I was a perfect candidate.

There were an estimated 12,000 patients in this country alone who were ready applicants for Betaseron. The number of people who were candidates, however, far exceeded the prepared number of dosages that were available. Therefore, in the beginning, Betaseron was dispersed on a lottery basis. Those with the higher number were first to receive the medication. I found that Dr. Hilbrandt was not only progressive in his treatment of MS but aggressive. He registered me in the program immediately, and I was fortunate enough to draw number 1,741 from of the original twelve thousand applicants.

Betaseron is administered by an injection subcutaneously (under the skin) every other day. When I first gave myself the injection, I did not have the convenience of an auto-injector as I do now, but I knew all too well that the consequences of not giving myself the shot more than outweighed the small skin prick that I felt!

What a life-changing breakthrough for those with multiple sclerosis! For me, this was the first time since my illness was diagnosed that I felt such freedom! Until now, from my first thought in the morning until my last consciousness at night, MS was in the forefront of my mind. My greatest fear was the eventual exacerbation that would permanently disable me. I lived with that foreboding thought constantly.

Now with the Betaseron injections, I felt totally liberated, free from the invisible shackles that bound me. I no longer second guessed my every move. I was celebrating each new day, believing that my health would remain constant.

As the months went by, I became less concerned with my MS and more occupied with other activities. What a wonderful feeling of independence! I was able to work again without the fear of overextending myself and having a relapse. For the first time in over seven years, I felt like a whole person once more. I accepted the permanent loss of some functions, but compared to where I was less than a decade ago, my life was moving in a positive direction again.

# CHAPTER FORTY-FOUR

*October 1998*

IT WAS RUMORED that Don's company would be relocating its entire facility to Greenville, South Carolina. By week's end, a memo confirmed the story to be true. The company's decision took everyone by surprise. The local news picked up the story that evening before we had time to even call our son at college. Poor DJ found out about the move on the local news.

"Do we really want to move again?" Don asked me the same night the news was confirmed. DJ was a junior at Virginia Tech and we really liked the area. Finally, we decided that if he could find employment locally, we would stay in Virginia. Don put out some feelers in the Roanoke Valley and actually accepted a position.

In the end though, we decided to move back to Pennsylvania. Don was offered a position with a company in the southeastern part of the state. After much to-do with the sale of our house in Virginia, we finally closed that door and moved our family back to Pennsylvania.

We felt badly, though, about leaving DJ in Virginia. He had another year at Virginia Tech before he could move north with us. Don's parents were not traveling much anymore, so it seemed like the right choice from their stand point. Another new address would be written on this year's Christmas cards.

I was managing the biweekly Betaseron injections for six years now, and I remained virtually symptom-free. My flare ups were minor compared to the first years of my illness, and I came to know exactly what would trigger an exacerbation and controlled my activities accordingly. I had faith in the Betaseron, although I never pushed my body to the limit. As Dr. Rosner stated in his book, "I am optimistic that a cure is only five to ten years away . . ." I believe that for those of us who are able to take advantage of the arresting qualities of Betaseron, we have our "cure", for now anyway.

With the assiduousness that I have always tried to maintain throughout the course of my illness, I hoped that I could stay a step ahead of the monster within me. I tolerated the Betaseron well, so I knew that I had a miracle in my pocket if I remained diligent.

# CHAPTER FORTY-FIVE

*December 1999*

THE MILLENNIUM WAS fast approaching, and the world seemed crazed with concerns about everything from the state of the banking system to the stock market and to the registers in our favorite stores going haywire at the stroke of midnight, 2000! Orson Welles's 1938 radio broadcast, *The War of the Worlds* came to mind. I hoped that by the final hours of 1999, the people would remain level-headed about the change. As it happened, nothing catastrophic occurred.

For our family, however, that first morning of the new millennium brought deep sorrow. At seven o'clock on the first of January, Pop called to tell us that Don's mom had passed away sometime during the night! He lost his voice several times as if his own words made no sense to him; why was he speaking in the past tense about the woman with whom he had shared the past fifty-eight years?

"I went upstairs to take Mom her shot of insulin . . . ," he paused again before he could continue, "She was gone, Bon . . ." The words seemed too foreign for him to finish his sentence.

I pictured Dad at this very moment, sitting on the small chair by their hall phone. The man, always sure-spoken and in control, was now reduced to an empty shell. The echoing quality of his voice cut through me as if a knife slowly shredded my heart. I turned to Don and wordlessly handed him the phone. He knew by my expression and the timing of the call that the news was bad.

"Dad?" Don said. His expression in the next few minutes broke my heart. I knew the pain of losing my mother, and I could feel the anguish that he was experiencing. "What happened?" he continued. It was obvious that he was trying to hold together for his father's sake. Finally, it was decided that they would talk in a few hours after they both came to grips with Mom's death.

Don's mom battled diabetes for years, and as she aged, it progressed to the point that she was receiving over double her normal dose of insulin. I assumed that her diabetic condition was responsible for what happened to her.

Mom was a spiritual person, one of the most devout individuals I have ever known. She took her faith seriously and lived a truly Christian life. I cannot recall a time when she had a malicious thought or word about anyone.

I remember a confrontation that she had once with her family doctor. He clearly was not listening to her concerns and helping her with her arthritis, so she decided that it was time to make a change.

When she left this office for the last time, she told me, "I was so angry with him, Bon. Do you know what I did?" I thought at last she had told this physician what she thought of him. "When I walked out of his office, I turned and stuck my tongue out at the closed door!" This was the most spiteful thing she could think to do!

Mom passed away in her sleep with a rosary in her hands. How often she would tell me that she hoped when her time came, she would pass in her sleep. Her prayers were answered. I am blessed to have known this remarkable lady for almost thirty years.

# CHAPTER FORTY-SIX

*March 2003*

WITHIN THE YEAR after Mom's passing, Dad decided to sell the house that he and Mom had shared for close to sixty years. It was too much for him to care for alone. There were many happy memories in their home, but he was ready to modify his lifestyle. He found a wonderful little apartment in a complex where some of his old friends also lived. He enjoyed the camaraderie of having his neighbors just a few steps down the hall. His power scooter provided him with the mobility to visit them anytime.

I remember calling late one evening and not being able to reach him. When I finally did get in touch with him the following day, he told me that he did not get back to his apartment until almost one in the morning!

"I was just visiting with some friends." he told me with a laugh.

Dad and I developed a special relationship through the years. He would introduce me to his friends as the daughter he had waited twenty-seven years for. When the boys were young and would do some dastardly damage in the house, I would just call Dad. He would come over to the house and fix it before their father came home from work! I remember when he had to repair the hinges on the dryer door after a rousing game of hide and seek when Brian tried to climb into the dryer to hide from his two brothers. There was also the time that a chipmunk ran into the house after someone left the front door open! Dad came to the rescue. He set up an elaborate maze to coax the chipmunk through the rooms until it reversed its direction and found its way back outside again.

After he moved to his apartment, Dad visited us at least twice a year. Don drove to Pittsburgh and picked him up for the holidays and also for his visit during the summer months. Dad and I would spend the day together, running errands or just sharing thoughts and stories.

He loved to reminisce about the times he spent as a boy in Pittsburgh. I enjoyed hearing about his numerous jobs as a youth (stripping the "stings" from celery stalks). He shared many anecdotes with me, including a family secret which I will take to my own grave.

One Monday afternoon, when they could not reach Dad by phone, his friends went to his apartment. He took his car for inspection in the morning, ate lunch, and then sat in his favorite recliner to rest. We received the call around dinnertime. Like Don's mom before him, he quietly passed in his sleep. I felt as if I had lost my own father all over again.

# CHAPTER FORTY-SEVEN

*September 2003*

MY HEALTH CONTINUED to remain balanced but for a slight overall decline that only I was able to measure from day to day. DJ and Sean both graduated from college and moved back home with us. Brian, who was starting his sophomore year at Penn State, took us by surprise when he announced that he was taking a semester off from college and joining the National Guard!

Neither his father nor I were thrilled by this decision, but he was nineteen years old and had made up his mind about the military before we were ever informed. This was the same little boy who would march through the house as a four-year-old using a mop handle as a prop for the real rifle he hoped to carry one day, so we weren't that surprised.

"Brian, do they know how bad your asthma is?" I asked him.

"They don't know," he answered in a cryptic tone of voice. Our son was ready to refute any argument we made on the subject of his enlistment. He planned to skip his spring semester for Basic Training.

Brian would be in Basic Training for the next sixteen weeks. He left on January 3, 2004, for Fort Knox, Kentucky. Our country was engaged in a war in the Middle East and there was no doubt that his deployment would follow immediately upon his graduation from training.

Nothing more was said about his medical condition. He hid it well, and the military was unaware of how severe my son's asthma could be if untreated. I remember many nights when I sat up with Brian when he had a bad attack. He was only nine months old, and I can still envision him lying on our bed at midnight, pulling his mouth open with his small fingers, trying to get air into his lungs. He was too young to understand why he could not breathe. That was the first of many trips to the emergency room.

These are the memories that a mother carries with her. I saw firsthand what could happen if Brian had an attack and did not have his inhaler with him. Now he was going to be without his medications and expending tremendous physical exertion.

His last week in the field was known as the FTX (Field Training Exercise). It is a 10K march out, conducting "missions" and training, sleeping in the field, and then a 15K trek back. Each private carries approximately one hundred pounds of gear for this training mission. The evening before he left for this final test, he called us. I could tell he was struggling to talk on the phone because he was in the throes of an asthma attack and he had no inhaler to use. Tomorrow, he would be conducting the most rigorous exercise of his sixteen weeks of training!

With divine intervention, Brian made it through the FTX and graduated on April 23, 2004. Soon after his release from Basic Training, his orders arrived.

He was being deployed to Camp Shelby, Mississippi, for the beginning of an eighteen-month deployment that would take him to the Middle East. What would happen when he was in full combat and had no means of controlling his asthma?

In the end, before he would leave for Mississippi, his pulmonary problems were discovered by his superiors and he was ordered to have another physical evaluation. This time, they realized the severity of his condition and recognized that Brian would not be able to endure the extreme heat and dryness of the desert.

Brian would eventually receive a full honorable discharge from the National Guard and would go on to finish his college education.

## CHAPTER FORTY-EIGHT

WHEN BRIAN LEFT for college, Rocky missed him terribly. He had been his constant companion since Brian was in fifth grade. One afternoon as I brushed Rocky, I discovered a lump on his side. I called our vet who saw him early the following morning. She confirmed our worst fears. Rocky was diagnosed with a Basal Cell Tumor.

This is a type of tumor that affects dogs, and although not always malignant, unfortunately for Rocky, this was not the case. The doctor explained that because we found it early, he had a good chance of survival. After surgery to remove the mass, the doctor gave Rocky a good prognosis.

Nine months after he was diagnosed with the cancer, Rocky fell ill again, only this time, he could not keep any food down. Within a day or so, he stopped eating entirely. Sadly, we knew that the end was near. We were grateful to have had these last months with him. Rocky was finally put to sleep on a Thursday evening after a last valiant effort to save him.

Brian was still in the military, but we knew that he would want to know about his old friend. We were unable to place the call to him, so when he got in touch with us that weekend, we told him what happened.

"Brian, Rocky got very sick late last week," I began in a hesitant voice. Don finished my sentence. "We finally had to have him put to sleep, Bri . . . the vet did everything possible, but we couldn't save him. We're so sorry."

There was dead silence on the line. Understandably, Brian could not speak for a minute, and we waited until he found his composure.

We went on to explain what happened, how Don and I sat on the floor the night before we took him to the vet's office for the last time. We fed him water with an eyedropper for hours, counting the cc's as we tried to get him to drink.

Before we ended the call, we assured our son that we had done everything possible to save his dog. We kept his ashes and made a shadow box with his collar, tags, and favorite toy. Since Brian was unable to be home for Rocky's last days, we felt that in this way, he would feel a part in the passing of his childhood pet.

The week after we had Rocky put down, Brian's friend Jayme called me. "We can't have Brian come home to an empty house!" she said to me. She was already thinking of replacing Rocky before Brian returned.

"Only if you can find a full bred German shepherd at the shelter," I heard myself saying to her, "then call me." I felt fairly certain that this would be a safe request. Two days later, Jayme called back to say that she found two shepherds at the shelter and asked if I wanted to meet her there.

I guessed wrong about the supply of German shepherds evidently. The workers had quarantined one of the dogs, so he was no longer being offered for adoption. The other, however, was a male who someone had found along the road and brought into the shelter.

He was a small, black, emaciated-looking dog. At first, he was very skittish so we took him into the visitor's area to see how he reacted on a one-to-one basis. As soon as I held a dog biscuit in my hand, the dog came over to my chair, sat in front of me, and gave me his paw! Of course, I melted. We tried a few more commands with him and realized that this dog must have come from a home where he was already socialized in a family environment.

The people at the shelter confirmed that he was found by the side of the road the week before and must have wandered from his property. No one had come forth to claim him so he was now eligible for adoption,

I still thought that the decision to find another dog should be Brian's. Maybe he didn't want to replace Rocky yet. He really would not be home to bond with a new pet as he had with Rocky. In the end though, I returned to the shelter and adopted the dog.

What was I thinking? This poor animal was solid black, his ribs showing, and his fur dull. He looked as if he had been homeless for a lot longer than a week. He certainly did not resemble Rin Tin Tin, and if Don was expecting a handsome German shepherd, this would not be the case (and it would cost me a hundred dollar fee if we chose to return the animal!).

All that being said, home we came with this gaunt, half-starved dog. Don was in the driveway when we pulled up. The dog leaped from my vehicle as soon as I opened the door. I saw Don's expression at the sight of this scruffy, malnourished dog and thought, "Uh oh!" but the pup ran right to Don and jumped up to make his acquaintance.

Don began to call him "Baron" (I hoped it would not take on Baron the Destructor's demeanor), and seven years later, Baron II is lying right next to me as I type! He turned out to be a wonderful and good-looking dog, a gentle giant weighing a bit shy of a hundred pounds!

Although Brian was thrilled when he returned from the military to find Baron, and it did help to ease his sorrow about losing Rocky, he would never bond with the dog as he had with his first dog. Don, on the other hand, is Baron's best friend. He practically eats from the table with us each evening!

# CHAPTER FORTY-NINE

BY THE END of 2007, I was beginning to see a decline in my cognitive skills. I finally left my job because of it. Even though it is part of the natural progression of multiple sclerosis, this frightened me as much as any physical inabilities. I knew from my extensive research of MS that there is no medication that will stop the deterioration of one's mental faculties caused by MS. Alzheimer drugs like Aricept are prescribed to help slow the advancement, but there is nothing to prevent it from happening.

I try to keep my mind as sharp as possible by doing crossword puzzles, reading, remembering lists, anything to ward off memory decline and the confusion that I feel at times. The loss of my reasoning and perceptive skills bothers me, and I wonder how long my cognitive problems can be veiled by a witty remark when I attempt to carry on a conversation and simple words elude me. This is a part of MS that many people do not recognize or understand.

I never aspired to be an Olympic medalist or to study ballet at The Juilliard School. My dreams were not quite that lofty. I've achieved most of what I have desired in my lifetime, and now, as

I watch my three children begin their own lives as adults, I am grateful to know that my illness did not interrupt the plans of these three amazing young men.

Don and I promised one another so long ago that we would never allow this disease to interrupt our life together or that of our children. We held onto that pledge, and I believe that it is one of the reasons that our sons will be able to accept the changes that will occur in their own lives. It made them stronger adults. They learned to cope with adversity at a very early age and then to move past it. In a way, MS qualified them to live in an ever-changing world and to accept the circumstances that they may encounter. I believe that it taught them the skills needed to move forward with their own personal relationships and careers.

As I reflect on all the transformations in my life, the decisions made in over two decade's time, I see that they all blended together and tightly secured our strong family bonds. It was a nomadic journey of sorts, given our diverse lifestyle at times.

My husband and sons, all my crazy pets, the places we've lived, and the people we've met, all combined to create a lifetime of joy, sorrow, intrigue, calamity, and lastly, rich fulfillment and love. For the most part, I am able to put multiple sclerosis on a shelf and only dust it off to teach a lesson or make a point.

But for the grace of God, family, friends, and fortitude, I grew to accept my challenges with multiple sclerosis. I've won more battles than I've lost with this disease. In the twenty-four years since my diagnosis, I have learned to accept whatever I am dealt because I know that in my life's plan, I am very blessed. This is not a calamitous death sentence. I will grow old and watch my children and grandchildren learn the ways of the world just as their father and I have done.

I don't know what the future will bring. I harbor no misgivings about the course or outcome of my life with multiple sclerosis. For me, the good things far outweigh the misfortunes of this illness. As my dying father was being wheeled into surgery, his last words to me were "What will, be will be." I live by that affirmation.

# *EPILOGUE*

AS THE AUDIENCE filed out of the auditorium this evening, I stood by the open door to shake their hands and bid them good night. They are my inspiration. I look at the joy and new belief that they are taking with them.

My wish for them, as with all those to whom I have shared my story, is always the same – as the days, months, and years of their lives unfold, I hope they will become stronger, more positive, genuinely happy individuals. I want them to put multiple sclerosis in its place and move on. I have done this in my own struggle with MS. In almost a quarter century since my diagnosis, I have come to terms with the illness, and although it has changed my life in some ways, I still hold on to the fundamental person who I was before I heard the words "You have multiple sclerosis."

Moving a mountain must begin with the toss of the first stone.

BCL

Email: *bmclein@gmail.com*

Website: *www.MSCares.net*

Title: ***My Story: A Personal Journey***

I WAS DIAGNOSED with multiple sclerosis in 1987. Since that time, many have asked me about my illness, and I have shared numerous stories about the challenges that I face with this disease.

When my son created *The Team 24/Seven Foundation* in honor of the twenty-fourth anniversary of my diagnosis, I decided that it was time to compile our many experiences as a family who learned to cope with the day-to-day challenges of MS.

*My Story: A Personal Journey* tells a sometimes humorous tale of the strength we, as a family, drew from one another to live productive lives despite trying times along the way. Three sons, numerous pets, and several moves combine to lend a lighthearted view of a devastating illness.

Much of the published information about multiple sclerosis does not touch on the human dynamics of the disease. I hope that by reading my experiences, I can be an inspriration to others who are battling with MS.

My husband and I reside in Pennsylvania with our German shepherd, Baron and our Yorkshire terrier, Finnegan.